Narrative Practice and Exotic Lives:

Resurrecting diver[illegible]ay life

by

Michael White

Dulwich Centre Publications
ADELAIDE, SOUTH AUSTRALIA

Chapter Two, 'Journey metaphors', was originally published in the 2002 No.4 issue of *The International Journal of Narrative Therapy and Community Work.*

Chapter Three, 'Folk psychology and narrative practice', was originally published in the 2001 No.2 issue of *The International Journal of Narrative Therapy and Community Work.*

Chapter Four, 'Narrative practice and the unpacking of identity conclusions', was presented at The Evolution of Psychotherapy Conference in Anaheim, California in May 2000, and was originally published in the 2001 Vol. issue of *Gecko: a journal of deconstruction and narrative ideas in therapeutic practice.* It was also published in Zeig, J.K. (ed) 2003: *The Evolution of Psychotherapy: A meeting of minds.* Phoenix: The Milton H. Erickson Foundation Press.

Chapter Five, 'Addressing personal failure', was originally published in the 2002 No.3 issue of *The International Journal of Narrative Therapy and Community Work.*

ISBN 0 9577929 9 9

Dulwich Centre Publications
Hutt St PO Box 7192
Adelaide 5000, South Australia
phone (61-8) 8223 3966, fax (61-8) 8232 4441
email: dcp@senet.com.au
website: www.dulwichcentre.com.au

Printed and manufactured by
Graphic Print Group, Richmond, South Australia.

Contents

Introduction

Dear Reader,

This book contains five of the papers that I have written over the past few years, and I am delighted that they have been brought together in this single volume. I am particularly pleased that this volume includes, as the first chapter, a paper entitled 'Narrative practice, couple therapy & conflict dissolution'. Couple therapy is a realm of therapeutic practice that is a common source of exasperation for many practitioners, and is a topic I have been intending to write about for a considerable time.

Chapter Two, 'Journey metaphors', provides an account of the significance of journey metaphors in narrative practice. This is an account of the ways that these metaphors can assist us to plot adventures in different domains of our working lives, and to achieve novel outcomes in the context of these adventures.

Chapter Three, 'Folk psychology and narrative practice', links many of the practices of narrative therapy to an historical tradition of understanding life and identity that is at times referred to as 'folk psychology'. Through detailed descriptions of therapeutic conversations and thorough explorations of history and culture, this chapter represents a call for the reinstatement of some of the understandings about human actions that are a feature of folk psychology.

Chapter Four, 'Narrative practice and the unpacking of identity conclusions', describes ways in which narrative practices can be employed to 'unpack' the negative conclusions that people who attend therapy have often formed about their identities and relationships. This chapter also describes the use of narrative practices in the rich development of conclusions about people's identities and relationships which displace these negative conclusions, and which provide a foundation for people to proceed with their lives.

The final chapter, 'Addressing personal failure', reviews the phenomenon of personal failure which has grown exponentially over recent decades – never before has the sense of being a failure to be an adequate person been so freely available to people, and never before has it been so willingly and routinely dispensed. This chapter describes in detail some of the operations of modern power that are associated with the dramatic growth of personal failure, and provides therapeutic options relevant to addressing this phenomenon.

It is my hope that these chapters will provide you, the reader, with sustenance, as you continue your own explorations of the extraordinary possibilities which arise in the context of therapeutic conversations.

The title for this book, *Narrative Practice and Exotic Lives: Resurrecting diversity in everyday life*, is linked to a sentiment proposed by social scientist/philosopher Pierre Bourdieu that has influenced my work for quite some time. Bourdieu proposes that one of the goals for those of us who wish to study our own familiar worlds is to 'exoticise the domestic'. On the subject of this sentiment, he states:

> *The sociologist who chooses to study his (sic) own world in its nearest and most familiar aspects should not, as the ethnologist would, domesticate the exotic, but, if I many venture the expression, exoticise the domestic, through a break with his (sic) initial relation of intimacy with modes of life and thought which remain opaque to him (sic) because they are too familiar. In fact the movement towards the originary, and the ordinary, world should be the culmination of a movement toward alien and extraordinary worlds.* (Bourdieu 1988, pp.xi-xii)

This notion of 'exoticising the domestic' has been of assistance to me in my efforts to characterise explorations of narrative practice. This seems entirely resonant with a form of therapeutic inquiry in which investigations of 'the ordinary world' culminate in investigations of 'alien and extraordinary worlds'.

This notion of 'exoticising the domestic' is a theme that links the papers in this volume. Amongst other things, these papers exoticise modern notions about the nature of life and identity that are considered to be universally true, generally relevant, and globally applicable. They also exoticise unquestioned cultural practices that are instrumental in inciting people to bring their lives into harmony with the socially constructed norms of contemporary western culture. And, furthermore, the papers in this collection exoticise some of the taken-for-granted counselling conventions that have the potential to reproduce the very contexts that are generative of the problems and predicaments that people bring to therapy.

So much about modern rationality obscures, diminishes and marginalises diversity in modes of life and thought. As a consequence of this, people's lives are rendered routine and, in a great many circumstances, sub-ordinary. The sentiment associated with 'exoticising the domestic' can provide an antidote to these effects of this modern rationality by encouraging therapeutic inquiry into what is unique in people's lives. In the context of inquiry shaped by this sentiment, the territories of people's lives that are routinely considered lacklustre and monotonous are rendered exotic. And in the context of inquiry shaped by this sentiment, therapeutic conversations that might otherwise reproduce the known and the familiar, become journeys to destinations that cannot be specified or predicted in advance of arrival.

This sentiment associated with 'exoticising the domestic' sponsors a form of therapeutic inquiry in which people suddenly find themselves interested in novel understandings of the events of their lives, curious about aspects of their lives that have been forsaken, fascinated with neglected territories of their identities, and, at times, awed by their own responses to the predicaments of their existence. For therapists, this sentiment fosters a consciousness of the life-shaping aspects of therapeutic inquiry, including a consciousness of the ways in which we, as therapists, are becoming other than who we were at the outset of our meetings with the people who consult us. This consciousness contributes significantly to the rich story development of our own lives and work, and can be a source of inspiration.

I welcome you to the papers included in this book that provide an account of therapeutic explorations I believe to be resonant with this sentiment. I hope that you will join me in working to further develop therapeutic practices that have the potential to 'exoticise the domestic', that will contribute to the identification of 'extraordinary worlds', and that will cultivate the resurrection of diversity in everyday life.

Michael White

Reference

Bourdieu, P. 1988: *Homo Academicus.* California: Stanford University Press.

chapter one

Narrative practice, couple therapy and conflict dissolution

Couple therapy

Some time ago I was speaking to a colleague who had been away from Adelaide for several years and who, upon returning, had opened an independent counselling practice. During our conversation I asked him how things were going in his new practice, and he responded with: 'Things were pretty torrid at the beginning. I wasn't having a very good time of my work. I felt quite daunted and overwhelmed, and was experiencing significant doubts about my decision to launch into this initiative. However, I went through a turning-point a couple of months ago, and since that time things have been working out much better, and I am now comfortable with the decision I made about this independent practice initiative.'

I was curious. This turning-point had obviously been very significant. What had contributed to this? In response to my questions, my colleague informed me that everything had changed for him when another therapist had leased an office across the corridor from his practice. I was interested to know why this development had so significantly contributed to the turning-point that my colleague had mentioned. In response to my question about this, my colleague said: 'Guess'. I had already assumed that this independent practice initiative may have been difficult for my colleague on account of the isolation that is frequently experienced by solo practitioners, and that the arrival of this other therapist had provided my colleague with an avenue for conversations about shared work interests and perhaps about some of the dilemmas and predicaments that they were facing in their respective therapeutic practices. It was my guess that they had been able to draw confirmation and support from each other in this. This assumption shaped my response: 'Well, was it that this development provided you with an option to meet to talk about your experiences of your work with each other, or for actual collaboration around your shared work interests?'

In response, my colleague said: 'Oh, no. We are very different people coming at our work from very different places with very different ideas which I doubt are compatible.' Now guessing that this connection was totally social, perhaps providing the opportunity for them to at least momentarily step back from their work from time to time, perhaps over coffee or lunch, I responded with: 'Was it that this contact provided you with the option of more of a social connection during your working day, perhaps one that makes it possible for you both to take some respite from some of the more pressing issues of your work?' 'No way', my friend said, 'Our perspectives on life are worlds apart. I think that we would be hard pressed to find anything that we might have in common. I don't believe that it would work at all well for us to attempt to get together socially. Besides, we are both now too busy for this.' As my colleague still wasn't forthcoming on the context of this turning-point, I said: 'Okay, tell me then. How did this development feature in this turning-point? How did it contribute to you experiencing greater enjoyment in your work?' 'Oh, that!', exclaimed my colleague with a grin. 'It's actually very simple. From the time that this other therapist moved in I have been able to send all of the couples that are referred to me across the corridor, and this had made a world of difference!'

I have chosen to share this story because it is not at all unusual for counsellors to experience special difficulties in working with couples that are highly conflicted. Of course there are exceptions to this, but I can recall many conversations with therapists who find working with these couples to be a particularly fraught experience, one that is highly frustrating to them. In talking about their work with couples who are in high conflict, therapists often speak about being 'driven to distraction' by experiences that leave them discouraged and exhausted.

I am sure that many of the readers of this piece will be able to relate to aspects of this account of some of the hazards of working with couples who have been highly conflicted over long periods of their relationships. I am also sure that many of the readers of this piece will be able to relate to my friend's sentiment about couple counselling in such circumstances. Time and again I have met with couples that are highly conflicted, where there is minimal overlap in terms of how the partners construct each other's actions and identities, where mutual understanding of the events of life seems slim, and where there is very little sense of shared responsibility for addressing the conflicts and frustrations of their relationships. Frequently, in these circumstances, these patterns of conflict are reproduced from the outset of the first consultation. On these occasions it is common for therapists to find that things start off badly, then get worse, and then deteriorate yet further. It is not unusual for therapists to report that, at these times, they have felt a longing for the materialisation of an 'authentic' therapist who might join them and who might save the situation, or that they have found themselves undertaking a review of some of those other career options that were cast aside at an earlier time in their lives: 'Well, there was always the option of gardening'. The scene is set for therapists to experience an impasse in their work, one that does not seem resolvable, and one in which they will feel quite dispossessed of a sense of knowing how to proceed in their conversations with these couples. I have certainly experienced such impasses.

I believe that there is a context to the development of this impasse; that, to a significant extent, this impasse is the outcome of social and relational forces that displace therapists from preferred positions in their work with the people who consult them. When displaced from this position, we can no longer respond in the ways that we routinely do in our consultations. At these times we find ourselves dispossessed of those familiar knowledges and skills of practice that we can usually depend upon to guide us in our work. I believe that to render visible the contexts that contribute to the development of these impasses can be of assistance to us in our efforts to maintain our positions of choice in our work with couples. To this end, I will here review just a few of the forces that I believe to be highly significant in the development of such impasses when being consulted by couples who have a history of high conflict. First I will describe some of the social and relational forces associated with the rise of 'communication theory', and second I will describe some of those forces associated with the narrowing of the legitimate and authorised relational forms of contemporary western culture.

After reviewing these social and relational forces that contribute to such impasses in the context of couple counselling, I will provide an account of consultations with a couple, one in which some appreciation of these social and relational forces contributed to the possibility for me to do what I would routinely do in these circumstances – that is, establish therapy as a context for rich story development. The approach to working with couples that I will be describing here I have found to be consistently helpful in my consultations with couples that have a history of high conflict. Frequently, these are couples that appear to exhaust themselves in their efforts to communicate their understandings to each other. These couples are very often quite isolated. I have also employed this approach, with some modification, in my work with many other couples.

Communication theory

Relationship counselling in western culture is a relatively recent phenomenon. It was developed during the post World War Two era of *information* technology, which represented a paradigm shift in relation to pre World War Two technology, which was predominantly a *mechanical* technology. The principal focus of this mechanical technology was the development of machines that were increasingly sophisticated and efficient in doing the work that they were designed for. In this climate, during this era the metaphors drawn into the human sciences were significantly mechanical metaphors. On account of this, the pre-World War Two psychologies were mostly mechanical psychologies. In the context of these psychologies, human beings were constructed as sophisticated machines to whom mechanical principles could be applied; for example, many of these psychologies were associated with the proposal that, in response to human difficulties, this sophisticated human machine could be reversed and unwound back to the site of the problem. When whatever it was that was broken was found and fixed, the developmental journey of life could again proceed. In reviewing some of the dominant images of these mechanical psychologies, Levenson (1972) observed:

> *Fixation and regression are images of time stoppage and reversal. It is as though the gears of the machine have come to a stop, or spun hopelessly, without traction. Even after many years, like a rusty locomotive, one can oil the parts, re-stoke the fires, raise the steam and move on. Regression has even more the mechanistic clockwork image. One can go back, reverse the direction of movement – clearly an operation impossible in a time-oriented perspective.* (p.59)

Following World War Two, information became the primary focus of technology. This was a focus on the effective and efficient and accurate transmission and processing of information, on the means of this transmission, on the storage of this information, and on its retrieval. This emphasis on the processing of information displaced the emphasis on the processing of energy which was primary in the era of mechanical technology. According to Levenson, this new technology was one that emerged 'out of the military need for effective tracking devices for anti-aircraft guns ...' (p.51). In describing this shift in technological paradigms, he states:

> *The first would be the period of the work machines, beginning with the simplest lever and wheel, on to the internal combustion and jet engines. All work machines potentiate physical effort. Second is the period of the information machine, starting at the time of World War II. This is the period of electronic technology rather than work technology.* (p.50)

In accord with this shift in technological paradigm, many of the metaphors taken up into post World War Two developments in the human sciences were metaphors of information processing and communication. Human beings were now constructed in terms of information processing machines, and the emphasis in inquiry turned to how humans compute information, and to studies in the development of precision in control inputs. This contributed to the development of new understandings of human action, and of people's predicaments of life. For example, in citing neurosis, Levenson observed that this was 'not something to be *undone* but a failure to *steer* properly due to a lack of information', that 'therapy depends on correcting feedback, increasing information or clarifying misunderstanding', and that 'neurosis is not so much a breakdown in intrapsychic machinery as a failure of understanding, either between persons or between person and society.' (pp.61 & 65)

In the adoption of these metaphors from information technology by the human sciences, communication was accorded a high status. The development of specific communication skills was now considered a panacea for many of the difficulties of human life. This idea was nowhere more vigorously applied than to the area of difficulties experienced in couple relationships. The relationship problems of couples were newly understood to be the outcome of absent or insufficient communication or of poor or inadequate communication. The resolution of relationship difficulties was to be found in the development of more functional communication styles, and relationship counsellors were to become 'technicians' in the development, repair, and restoration of communication. They were assisted in this vocation through the concerted development of schemes for the measurement of and for the correction of communication. Such schemes enabled the rating of communication on continuums with 'masked', 'indirect', 'inaccurate', and 'dishonest' communication at one end, and 'open', 'direct', 'accurate' and 'honest' communication at the other. It was this open, direct, accurate and honest communication that was to be aspired to, for not only was this considered desirable, but 'healthy'.

Narrowing of legitimate relational forms

In the recent history of western culture, it has been the heterosexual married couple that is privileged over all other relational forms. Not only is this privileged as the ideal relational form, but many other relational forms have been consistently downgraded, discouraged, marginalised, disqualified and punished. Some historians have traced the history of this circumstance and, when reviewing the trajectory of the modern heterosexual marriage, have concluded that the privileging of this form is the outcome of a narrowing of the legitimate and authorised relational forms over the past several centuries.

For example, according to Foucault's (1994) accounts of life in the pre-Christian Hellenistic and Roman worlds, historically there were other modes of relationship, like friendship, that were recognised and institutionally privileged. These were modes in which not only the benefits and rewards of relationship were acknowledged, but in which a range of obligations, tasks, and reciprocal duties were to be observed:

> *Take, for example, notions of friendship. They played an important part, but there was a supple institutionalised framework for them – even if it was sometimes constraining – with a system of obligations, tasks, reciprocal duties, a hierarchy between friends, and so on. I don't think we should reproduce that model. But you can see how a system of supple and relatively codified relations could exist for a long time and support a certain number of important and stable relations, which we now have great difficulty defining. When you read an account of two friends for the period, you always wonder what it really is ...* (p.159)

As an outcome of this narrowing of the legitimate, institutionally authorised, and acknowledged relational forms, Foucault concludes that today we 'live in a legal, social, and institutional world where the only relations possible are extremely few, extremely simplified, and extremely poor' (1994, p.158).[1] This narrowing of relational forms has given rise to the development of high exclusivity in couple relationships. This is an exclusivity in which partners in relationships that conform with what is institutionally authorised are increasingly expected to be everything to each other. It is one that privileges the orthodox couple relationship to the extent that it fosters the exclusion of, or the diminishment of the significance of, other relational forms in the development of one's life and identity. This is an exclusivity that requires partners to look solely to each other in their efforts to find solidarity in regard to the range of intentions and purposes of one's life, in their search for communion in all of one's values and beliefs, and in one's endeavour to satisfy every desire and longing. This is an exclusivity that is associated with the idea that partners can expect to find in each other the totality of whatever it is that provides the foundation for their existence.

These observations about the narrowing of the legitimate, authorised, and acknowledged relational forms do not constitute an assertion about a lack of diversity in relational forms in the contemporary world. And they do not constitute a disqualification of the many present endeavours to forge new relational forms, and to achieve legitimacy for these. However, these observations are associated with a recognition of the powerful social, economic, political, legal, and ideological forces that are at play that contribute to the downgrading and disqualification of these other relational forms, and that incite heterosexual couples to embrace exclusivity in their relationships. These forces also incite non-heterosexual couples to emulate this exclusivity in order to achieve at least a small grant of normative worth in this contemporary world.

Consequences for couple life

The rise of communication theory and the narrowing of the legitimate and authorised relational forms has had significant effects on couple life.

The promotion of healthy communication

What are the consequences, to couple life, of the adoption of these metaphors from information technology? What are the consequences of understanding difficulties in couple relationships to be the outcome of absent, insufficient, poor, or inadequate communication? And what are the consequences of the notion that more communication, and its further development, would be a panacea for the difficulties experienced in couple relationships?

The consequences of these developments are manifold, and I will review just a few of them here. First, these developments encourage couples to persist in efforts to principally achieve conflict resolution and problem negotiation through communication. Upon the occasion of these efforts bearing little fruit, or in the face of a deteriorating situation as an outcome of these efforts, these understandings about communication and relationship difficulty inspire couples to further renew their efforts at conflict resolution and problem negotiation through communication – to engage in doing more of the same. Invariably the consequence of this is misery, and a conclusion that the relationship is a failure and/or that the partners are incompetent.

Second, this investment in communication per se as a remedy for relationship difficulties obscures the extent to which communication is associated with the making of meaning. The act of communication is not a neutral act – in the act of communicating with each other about relationship difficulties partners are constructing each other's identity, and the identity of their relationships. For example, in the context of efforts to resolve difficulties through direct communication, partners can be not only confirming the negative conclusions that they hold about each other's identity and about the identity of the relationship, but further constructing these negative identity conclusions. The further development of these negative conclusions has significant shaping effects on relationships, contributing to complications that can become increasingly insurmountable over time. However, because this making of meaning is obscured by the notion of communication as remedy, and because the consequences of this meaning-making remains relatively invisible to couples in these contexts, it becomes very difficult for partners to assume any responsibility for these negative developments in their relationship.

Third, this emphasis on communication as a panacea for relationship difficulties neglects the fact that couple relationships are rarely level playing fields. There are many imbalances of power in couple relationships. In heterosexual relationships, many of these imbalances are of the politics of gender. On account of this power differential, it can be quite unsafe for women partners to speak openly of what they think and feel; as an outcome of open, direct and honest communication some people can find themselves being subject to acts of retribution from their partners that are further subjugating of them.

Fourth, because the style of communication fostered by these metaphors from information technology is adopted as the norm for healthy communication, the ethno/cultural-, socio-economic-, class- and era-centred location of this norm is masked. This formula for appropriate communication is held to be universally relevant to all peoples, in all places, in all cultures, in all classes, in all socio-economic circumstances, and in all times. However, all proposals for living are historical and cultural products, and the particular relational style that is championed in this assertion about what constitutes healthy communication reflects the ideals of the privileged middle/upper middle-class western white culture of the modern era. On account of this assertion about what constitutes healthy communication, in response to difficulties in couple relationships, partners are encouraged to more closely emulate the cherished mainstream lifestyle norms of modern contemporary culture, and to discount a diversity of practices of conflict resolution and problem negotiation that are of their more intimate histories, and that are culture-, class- and location-specific.

In describing some of the potential hazards of modern notions about communication as a panacea for the difficulties experienced in relationships, it has not been my intention to suggest that communication is a bad idea, or that the relational style promoted by modern notions about healthy communication is wrong. No doubt there are many couples who will find this relational style to be in harmony with their cultural, socio-economic and class location, and for whom this version of addressing relational difficulties will be effective. However, in the forgoing discussion it has been my intention to render modern taken-for-granted notions of healthy communication 'exotic', and to address some of the pitfalls associated with these notions. Although such pitfalls have been highlighted by other writers at different times, the notion that this communicational style is a panacea for the difficulties of relationships is one that is still strongly held in modern times, and one that is highly influential in shaping partners' responses to difficulties experienced in couple relationships.

Narrowing of relational forms

What are the consequences of the narrowing of the legitimated, authorised and acknowledged relational forms? What are the consequences of the privileging of the heterosexual marriage as the ideal relational form? And what is the outcome of the exclusivity that is fostered in this development?

This exclusivity that incites partners to look solely to each other in their efforts to find solidarity in regard to the range of intentions and purposes of one's life, in their search for a sense of communion in all of one's values and beliefs, and in one's endeavour to satisfy every desire and longing, is profoundly isolating of couples. Any initiatives to engage with other relational forms in this quest draw negative sanctions, and the outcome of this is the deferment of much that is precious to each partner, or the development of covert avenues in the pursuit of this quest.

In these circumstances, relationships can so easily be failed. This sense of failure often arises in relation to actions that are constructed as betrayal and, in the context of this exclusivity, so many actions can be constructed in this way – for example, even the sharing of a confidence with a person outside of the relationship that is not shared with a partner is perceived to be a betrayal, and is considered to reflect negatively on the relationship itself. In the context of exclusivity, where any measures that a partner may take in order to hold something private is negatively construed as an act of secrecy, the spectre of the failing relationship is ever-present. For many couples, the idea that partners can expect to find in each other the totality of whatever it is that is to provide the foundation for their existence, furnishes a sense of ongoing distress and desperation, and for the personal experience that is commonly referred to as jealousy.

I have reviewed some of the isolating effects of modern exclusivity, and the propensity of this exclusivity to sponsor the phenomenon of betrayal and jealousy, and conclusions about relationship failure. Apart from these consequences, it is also apparent that the high privilege that is allocated to the ideal of the modern couple relationship, and particularly to the heterosexual marriage, is also narrowing of this very relational form. In that this exclusivity insulates partners from other relational forms, and from appreciating the viability and relevance of these other relational forms in the pursuit of one's quests in life and in the resolution of one's relationship conflicts, it restricts their opportunity to incorporate aspects of these other relational forms in their couple relationships. It is in this way that this exclusivity contributes not just to an erosion of diversity in relational forms, but to an erosion of diversity within the couple relationship itself.

In drawing out some of the consequences of the modern exclusivity of couple relationships, it has not been my intention to suggest that this exclusivity does not work for some couples at some times, or that this should not be aspired to. Rather, I have described some of the consequences of this modern exclusivity that have been so clearly apparent in the relationships of a great many of the couples who have consulted me over the years, and for whom challenging this exclusivity has been instrumental in the development of a satisfying relationship.

Consequences for therapy

The context of couple counselling is not exempt from these cultural assumptions about the cause of relationship difficulties, about the solution to these difficulties, and about the part that the counsellor will play in this. Couples frequently enter this context expecting to renew their efforts to address relationship difficulties through the performance of the revered communicational style of contemporary western culture, and with the expectation that they can be safe in the knowledge that the therapist will be able to mediate these efforts – I can't count the number of times over the years that I have heard, when meeting with couples, various renditions of: 'We have come here to vent and for you to fix what is broken'.

Therapists are not just vulnerable to these expectations that couples bring into counselling contexts, but they can also be powerfully influenced by the weight of parallel expectations that have their genesis in the history of relationship counselling. In these circumstances, therapists frequently abandon what they would usually do in their consultations with people who seek their help, and instead join couples in their efforts to do more of the same: in their efforts to address their relationship difficulties through this revered communicational style. In joining with couples in this way, the therapist assumes a responsibility to assist them to close the gap between what they have achieved in regard to communication and the ideals for couple communication, between their location on the various continuums of communication, and the 'healthy' polarities of these continuums.

Although at times, when joined with couples in this way, therapists do become aware that they have been unwitting accomplices in the further construction of negative identity conclusions which are shaping of developments in couple relationships, the part that the partners are playing in this invariably remains invisible to couples. This further limits options for couples to assume responsibility for these constructions of each other's identity, and to recognise the consequences of these constructions in the shaping of their relationships.

Not only do cultural assumptions about communication have the potential to powerfully influence what is done in the name of relationship counselling, but so does the assumption of exclusivity. Counselling can be perceived, by couples, as a context in which they will intensify their efforts to become everything to each other; to look to each other in their efforts to find solidarity in regard to the range of intentions and purposes of one's life, in their search for communion in all of one's values and beliefs, and in one's endeavour to satisfy every desire and longing. Therapists are not just vulnerable to these expectations of couples, but also to a time-honoured tradition in couple counselling in which the couple relationship is entirely centred in initiatives to address relationship difficulties; in which the focus of all initiatives to address relationship difficulties is entirely on the couple itself. When therapists centre couples in this way, they can become unwitting accomplices in the exacerbation of this modern exclusivity; in limiting options for the partners to explore alternative relational forms in the pursuit of their quests, and in further restricting the opportunity for couples to take up and incorporate other relational styles that might contribute to the development of diversity of response within the couple relationship itself. This sets the scene for renewed experiences of betrayal and desperation.

Implications of this analysis

These observations about the potential consequences, in the therapeutic context, of these cultural assumptions about relationship difficulties and about the solution to these difficulties, do not constitute a rejection of general practices of mediation in the context of couple therapy, or a questioning of the validity of setting the scene for partners of couple relationships to communicate openly and directly with each other about a range of matters. However, when consulted by couples in high and longstanding conflict, where there seems little overlap in terms of shared understandings of the events of their relationship, it can be very helpful for the therapist to question the assumption that the revered communicational style that I have described in this paper will be a panacea for relationship difficulties, and the assumption that therapeutic practices that reinforce the expectation of exclusivity in couple relationships will be beneficial.

In the next section of this paper I will provide an account of working with couples in high and longstanding conflict. This is an account of couple therapy that is disruptive of efforts to resolve difficulties in relationships through the sort of dialogue founded on contemporary ideas about good communication, and of counselling initiatives that are further centring of the couple relationship as the foundation of each partner's existence. An extended transcript of an interview with a couple will be used to illustrate this approach. Although a range of narrative practices will be reflected in this transcript, not all of these will be discussed. In regard to these practices, I will specifically focus on *definitional ceremony practices* and on the *repositioning* of the partner who is to assume the outsider-witness position in the context of these definitional ceremony practices.

As these definitional ceremony practices and this repositioning are critical to the success of this approach to working with couples in high and longstanding conflict, I will review both of these subjects before turning to the illustration of this approach.

Definitional ceremony

The definitional ceremony structure is a characteristic feature of narrative practice. I borrowed the metaphor 'definitional ceremony' from the work of cultural anthropologist, Barbara Myerhoff (1982, 1986). She employed this metaphor in her efforts to describe the identity projects of a community of elderly Jews in Venice, Los Angeles. I have written extensively on the relevance of this metaphor, and on the relevance of the structure of these identity projects, to therapeutic practice (for example, see White 1995, 1997, 1999). I will only provide a brief account of this here, and will begin by quoting from 'Reflecting-team work as definitional ceremony revisited' (White 1999):

> *The definitional ceremony metaphor guides the structuring of forums in which certain persons have the opportunity to engage in a telling of some of the significant stories of their lives – stories that, in one way or*

another, are relevant to matters of personal and relational identity. Also present in this forum is an audience or 'outsider-witness group'. The members of this group listen carefully to the stories told, and ready themselves to engage in a retelling of what they have heard. When the time is right, positions are switched – the persons whose lives are at the centre of the definitional ceremony form an audience to the retellings of the outsider-witness group. These retellings encapsulate aspects of the original telling. But more than this – these retellings of the outsider-witness group routinely exceed the boundaries of the original telling in significant ways, in ways that contribute to the rich description of the personal and relational identities of the persons whose lives are at the centre of the ceremony. In part, these retellings achieve this through the linking of the stories of the lives of these persons with the stories of the lives of others, around shared themes, values, purposes and commitments.

After these retellings, the members of the outsider-witness group step back into the audience position, and the persons whose lives are at the centre of the ceremony have the opportunity to speak of what they have heard. At this time these persons are engaged in the second of the retellings; that is, in retellings of retellings of the outsider-witness group. In these forums, there can be other levels of outsider-witness participation, and further retellings of retellings.

The definitional cerėmony metaphor guides the structuring of tellings and retellings of the stories of people's lives in uniquely convened social arenas. Within the context of these ceremonies, these tellings, retellings, and retellings of retellings are distinct. The achievement of these distinct tellings and retellings requires a disruption of dialogue across the interface between those in the audience position and those who are engaged in the tellings and retellings; that is, when the outsider-witness group is in the audience position, they are strictly in that position, and when the persons whose lives are at the centre of definitional ceremonies are in the audience position, they are strictly in that position. (pp.63-64)

The retellings of these definitional ceremonies are shaped by a specific tradition of acknowledgement. These retellings do not constitute a reproduction of the entire content of the telling that went before. Rather, in this tradition of acknowledgement, it is those aspects of the telling that outsider witnesses were most strongly drawn to that provide the foundation for this retelling. When the people who are in the outsider-witness position are unfamiliar with this tradition of acknowledgement, the therapist has a responsibility for the structuring of these retellings. In assuming this responsibility, the therapist usually conducts an interview of the outsider witnesses, one that is informed by specific categories of inquiry. This interview provides a scaffold that assists outsider witnesses to:

1. Identify and speak of the expressions of the telling that they were most drawn to. These are the expressions that most caught the attention of the outsider witnesses, that most captured their imagination, and that provided the outsider witnesses with a sense of what it is that the person accords value to in life. These expressions may be specific words or phrases, or particular moods and sentiments. In first speaking of the expressions that they were most drawn to, outsider witnesses signal that their interest in the person's life is particular interest, not general interest; defined interest, not global interest.

2. Describe the images that were evoked for them by these expressions. These images might take the form of certain metaphors about the person's life, or might take the form of mental pictures of the person's identity or of the identity of the person's relationships. At this time, outsider witnesses are encouraged to speculate about what these metaphors and mental pictures might reflect about the person's purposes, values, beliefs, hopes, dreams and commitments. Outsider witnesses are encouraged to express these reflections in the subjunctive mood of 'as if, may be, possibly, etc.'

3. Embody their responses to the telling by providing an account of why they were so drawn to these expressions. This is achieved by inviting the outsider witnesses to provide some account of why they were drawn to particular expressions of the telling, of what these expressions struck a chord with in their own personal history. In situating their interest in the person's expressions in the history of their own experiences of life, the interest of the outsider witnesses becomes embodied interest, not disembodied interest; personal interest, not academic interest; engaged and vital interest, not 'armchair' interest.

4. Acknowledge the ways in which they have been moved on account of being present to witness these expressions of life. 'Moved' here is employed in the

broad sense of this word. For example, outsider witnesses might speak about where this experience has taken them in regard to their own thoughts, including their reflections on their own existence, their understandings of their own lives, or their perspectives on life more generally. Or they might speak about where this experience has taken them in regard to speculation about conversations they might have with figures of their own life, or about options for action in regard to predicaments in their own lives and relationships. This acknowledgement provides an account of how the outsider witnesses have been touched in ways that have contributed to them becoming other than who they were on account of witnessing the person's expressions, and on account of having the opportunity to respond to the person's story by way of this retelling.

Following the retelling of the outsider witnesses, the therapist interviews the person whose life is at the centre of the ceremony according to the same four categories of inquiry, except that the focus of the second category of inquiry remains on the images of this person's life and identity, not on images of the life and identity of the outsider witnesses; that is, at this time, this person is usually interviewed about the metaphors or mental pictures of their *own* life that were evoked by the retellings of the outsider witnesses.

Re-tellings structured according to these categories of inquiry have the potential to be highly resonant for the people whose lives are at the centre of the definitional ceremony. It is this resonance that contributes very significantly to rich story development, to a stronger familiarity with what one accords value to in life, and to the erosion and displacement of various negative conclusions about one's life and identity. This provides a foundation for people to know how to proceed in their efforts to address the dilemmas and predicaments of their lives.

Repositioning

When interviews with couples are structured by definitional ceremony practices, the therapist interviews one partner (partner A) in the presence of the other partner (partner B) who is positioned as an outsider witness. In a subsequent meeting, the roles are reversed – the partner who was first interviewed (partner

A) is positioned as an outsider witness to an interview of the other partner (partner B).

It can be extraordinarily difficult for partners who are in significant dispute to reproduce the tradition of outsider-witness responses. It requires them to disengage from their routine and habitual ways of responding to each other. These routine and habitual responses seem almost hard-wired, and these can be very captivating of the partners in the midst of their efforts to respond to the stories of each other's lives. I believe that disengagement from these routine and habitual responses can be best achieved by inviting the partner who is to be the outsider witness to separate from a sense of being in his/her relationship for the duration of our meeting. This can be done by assisting this partner to adopt an alternative position, one from which they will find it easier to reproduce the tradition of outsider-witness response that is characteristic of definitional ceremony.

Thus, ahead of interviewing the partner who is to be at the centre of the definitional ceremony, the partner who is to undertake the outsider-witness role is interviewed in ways that assist them to separate from their relationship for the duration of the interview, and to reposition themselves in relation to their partner. This repositioning interview is usually prefaced by some discussion of the difficulties that can be predicted in efforts to respond, as an outsider witness, in ways that are not dictated by the usual habits of response that characterise one's relationship. It is also prefaced by some observations that, although some things can be achieved in the context of relationship that might not be achieved outside of this context, it is usually the case that some things can be achieved in the context of other relationship forms that might not be achieved in the context of couple relationships.

The repositioning interview then proceeds. In this interview, the partner who is to be the outsider witness (partner B) is invited to share stories about experiences of their life in which they have experienced significant acknowledgement, understanding, compassion or acceptance, and about the figures who extended this acknowledgement, understanding, compassion, or acceptance. These stories provide a foundation for a repositioning of partner B; partner B will be assisted to reposition themselves as one of these figures when in the outsider-witness position. It is important that the figure chosen by partner B is acceptable to partner A; Partner A has power of veto in this regard. The figure chosen by partner B would not be one that partner A has had a negative experience of, or feels alienated from in any way. There are occasions upon which the figure chosen will be of partner B's more distant history and not known to partner A. On these occasions it is important for partner A to have the opportunity to get a good sense of this person before sanctioning the choice of this figure as a foundation for the repositioning of partner B.

Ahead of initiating this inquiry, it is important to exclude partner A as a candidate who might be implicated in partner B's stories of acknowledgement, understanding, compassion or acceptance, for there is the hazard that this partner will feel slighted if not chosen, and will experience this as a disqualification of his/her contribution to the relationship and to partner B's life. Also, if partner A isn't excluded as a candidate, and, as a result, partner B positions themselves as partner A when in the outsider-witness position, the exercise can become very complex.

To facilitate this repositioning, the therapist interviews partner B in ways that contribute to these expressions of acknowledgement, understanding, love, compassion and/or acceptance becoming more richly known, and in ways that draw out the identities of the figures implicated in this. In the first place, it is usual for partner B to simply define these expressions as essentialist phenomena; to define these as expressions of a figure's inherent qualities or attributes (for example: 'Uncle X was a very compassionate sort of person'), or as quantitative phenomena (for example: 'Mrs. Smith was so full of love'). However, in the context of this repositioning interview, partner B is assisted to also define these expressions as specific and highly honed relationship skills; as time-honoured practices of living that can be known in their particularities; as a specialised know-how about building a sense of affiliation in relationships. As partner B becomes more familiar with the specifics of these skills in the repositioning interview, s/he can be invited to reflect upon what these suggested about the figure's sentiments of living; about this figure's perspective on life, and about their purposes, values and beliefs, etc.

The repositioning interview is drawn to a close when partner B believes that they have a strong familiarity with these relational skills and with the sentiments of living associated with these, and has signalled a readiness to step into the outsider-witness position for the interview with partner A. At this time partner A has power of veto over any of these skills and sentiments of life that s/he might have discomfort about. The therapist then informs partner B that s/he will do what they can to assist them maintain the position they have chosen (this might be friendship, brotherhood, sisterhood, uncle-hood, aunt-hood, parenthood, colleagueship, etc.), and reaches an agreement with partner B about how the therapist might interject should s/he believe that partner B is falling back into their relationship with partner A during any phase of the definitional ceremony. Further, partner B is informed that on these occasions they will be consulted about options for proceeding: about whether a simple reminder of the task at hand will be sufficient for them to re-engage with the chosen position; about whether to re-engage in the repositioning interview in ways that would contribute to greater familiarisation with the skills associated with the figure's expressions of acknowledgement or whatever, as well as this figure's sentiment of living; about whether to temporarily suspend the exercise in order to gain clarification on any hurdles to engaging with the chosen position, or to engage in explorations of what might make it more possible to assume this position; or to permanently abandon the exercise in order to pursue other approaches.

Point of entry

When consulted by couples in high and longstanding conflict, it is my usual practice to invoke definitional ceremony as a structure for our conversations. In regard to the question about which partner is first invited to place their life at the centre of the definitional ceremony, when there is a significant imbalance in the relationship in terms of power, this is usually the partner who is more in the subject position in the power relationship. When there is not this apparent imbalance, it is the opportunities for rich personal story development that first become visible to the therapist that determines which partner will be initially invited to occupy the centre of the definitional ceremony.

Usually, these opportunities for rich story development arise from expressions of conflict. These expressions of conflict take many shapes, and include the voicing of discontent and dissatisfaction, usually accompanied by ultimatums and repudiations; some aspect of the relationship that may have been accepted by one partner is no longer acceptable to them, and must be changed; some aspect of the relationship that has always been unsatisfactory is now even more so, and must be resolved; some ideas that one partner has about the other are 'off the wall', and just have to be straightened out; some of the expectations that one partner has about the role of the other are 'inappropriate', and if these are not modified the relationship will end; some of the actions that one partner negatively values are positively valued by the other as expressions of resistance, and so on. In all of these discontents, dissatisfactions, ultimatums and repudiations, can be found points of entry to the rich story development of the lives and identities of the partners of these couples.

For example, when a partner is giving voice to conclusions about what is no longer acceptable to them, or about what is no longer satisfactory to them, or about what is 'off the wall', or about the 'inappropriate' role expectations of the other, or about the negative effect of actions valued positively by the other, there is the opportunity to interview this partner about the foundation of these conclusions. For example, it can be assumed that these conclusions are the outcome of certain realisations that this partner has had about his/her life; perhaps about one's purposes in life, or about what sort of lifestyle one would find more suitable, or about one's preferred ways of being in life, or about one's personal worth, or about one's unrecognised capabilities, and so on. Further, it can be assumed that these realisations are the outcome of specific experiences of life, experiences that have contributed discoveries about and clarifications of what the partner accords value to in life. It is assumptions like these that provide a foundation for the sort of therapeutic inquiry that contributes to the rich development of the stories of people's lives.

In summary, it is usually specific relationship conflicts that provide the point of entry to the sort of rich story development that is a feature of narrative conversations with couples who have been in high and longstanding conflict. However, once begun, these conversations quickly drift away from relationship conflicts and instead provide the opportunity for the rich description and strong acknowledgement of developments in the lives of the respective partners, and of the relationship between these developments and what the partners hold precious about their lives; it is *not* the relationship conflicts, or the relationship per se that remain at the centre of these therapeutic explorations. I believe that the forthcoming story will provide clarification of how this might be done.

Couple therapy as definitional ceremony: an illustration

I entered the waiting room and introduced myself to a newly referred couple. The partners were not sitting together, and I sensed a degree of tension between them. Their introductions were perfunctory; they were clearly ill at ease. There seemed an awkwardness with which we negotiated the passageways to the interviewing room and, when seated, my efforts to make this couple feel more at home fell flat. I then noticed that each partner had pulled their chair a little further apart from each other, a movement that had taken place after being seated, although not one that I been aware of at the time. It was my guess that this couple had argued ahead of arriving at my office, and that this was about their attendance for the interview that we were about to have. Under these circumstances I thought it wise to inquire about the context of making the appointment to meet with me, and about the events leading up to our meeting in the waiting room.

Barry[*]: Well, to be honest, this is something that I have been wanting for a long time now. But I kept putting it off because I didn't think that my partner would agree to come with me to see you about our relationship. But in the end I just took the plunge and called to make a time, just hoping against hope that my partner would see the wisdom in such a meeting. But I'm apprehensive about this, and things have been pretty rough between us this morning before coming here. Pearce says I didn't consult him about the time of this meeting but you will find that he always tends to be a bit antagonistic when …

Pearce: Barry, I can't believe that you are saying this! Michael, I don't believe Barry is saying this! Of all the things that ... This just drives me nuts! Barry always does this. He is always taking credit for ideas that aren't his in the first place. This is a serious problem. For ages I've been working behind the scenes in my efforts to make this meeting happen, and Barry knows this. You know this Barry! Michael, he is such a contrary person that I just knew that I had to encourage him to take this initiative, to make this appointment, or he would never come. Sure, I left it to him to make the actual appointment, but I really didn't see any choice in this. But then this is the way that I have to

---

[*] All names are pseudonyms.

work at most things in our relationship, or nothing would ever happen. Barry's the sort of person who ...

Barry: You can't believe what I am saying!! I can believe what you are saying! I'm glad to see that you are being true to form Pearce. You are going to ruin this, aren't you. Michael, Pearce is just like his sister. She won't co-operate with anyone unless it is on her terms. Everything always has to be on her terms. Pearce, you know it, you are just like you sister. And I ...

Pearce: Hang on a minute. Just hang on! Can't we ever talk about our relationship without your dragging my family into it? Can't we just once, just once, have a simple discussion without you doing this? You're making it impossible. Michael, see, Barry has this thing about my family. This is the other big problem that we have. Barry, just why are you so preoccupied with my family!! It's not as if ...

Barry: That's not fair! And you know it! At least I relate to your family. I can't say that you return the favour. You know how hard I have tried with them, and how accepting I have been of your family even when you haven't even put an iota into ...

Pearce: Look, if this is how it is going to be, if this is how you are going to be, then I don't see the point of us going through this exercise. If this is how it is going to be, then I am out of here. It is not going to do anything ...

Barry: That's wild! Michael, I predicted that Pearce would do this. Pearce, you are just looking for an excuse. You want to pull the plug on this just because things are not working out in the way that you want them to. I can't accept this. Michael, I used to just put up with this sort of petulance, and just back off when the going got difficult like this. But I can't do it anymore, I just can't, and I don't know if ...

Pearce: So it's all about what is acceptable to you now, is it! Just in case you forgot, I'm in this relationship too you know!

M: (tentatively) Would it be okay for me to make a comment. Or would this be a bad time?

Barry: Sure! Sure!

Pearce: Sure, anything but this. I can't stand this.

M: I've appreciated your openness and your frankness. You have both been quite candid. I am not just a stranger to the two of you, but I am also a stranger to your relationship. But you have done a great job of catching me up with how things sometimes go for you in this relationship, and about what I guess you have come to consult me about. In circumstances like this, one picture has to be worth a thousand words. Or is it one performance is worth a thousand words?

Pearce: Okay, okay, I get it.

Barry: What? Oh, yeah.

M: In saying this, I'm not trying to bring about premature closure to this conversation that you are having, and I'd be prepared to keep listening to further developments in this if you thought that this would be instructive for me, and if you thought you were making some headway. But there is another option. If you think that you have given me at least a partial understanding of what you wanted to consult me about, if you think that you have achieved this, I have an idea about something else that we could try. This would be a different way of going about things. What do you think?

Pearce: Anything. Anything but more of this.

Barry: Yeah, I agree.

M: Okay then. Here is my proposal. I suggest that I interview you both separately, but in each other's company. If this idea appeals to you, we could do this in three parts. First, one of you would be an audience to my conversation with the other. Then, let's say about half-way through the interview, I could interview whichever of you who'd been in the listening position. I'd interview you about what you'd heard. I often refer to this as a 'retelling'. Towards the end of our meeting I would be asking whoever was first interviewed about their response to this retelling. Then, for our next meeting, I would start by interviewing whoever was in the audience position today, and the other partner would have a turn at listening. Now I know that this is not what you had expected in making this appointment to meet with me, but I have a sense that doing things in this way might assist us all to find a way forward in attending to what is so important to both of you. What do you think? Would you like to give this a try?

Pearce: Okay. It sounds interesting. I'll give it a go.

Barry: Yeah. When you think about it we've got nothing to lose. We'll be guided by you.

M: Okay, but it might not be all that easy to do this. So, we will have to make some preparations for it, because it is important for you to separate from your relationship for the duration of this exercise.

Pearce: What! But we came here to ...

M: I'm not suggesting that you separate from each other. I am just suggesting that you separate from your relationship with each other for the duration of each meeting that we have. There are many things that can be achieved in relationships that might not be achieved outside of them. But there are also things that can be achieved in friendship, in acquaintanceship, in cousinship, or whatever, that might not be achieved in the context of a relationship. If we are successful in finding another place for you to stand in relation to each other in the course of our conversations, there will be less chance that your responses to each other will be determined by how things usually go between the two of you. And there will be more chance that you will be free to respond to each other in ways that are not so predictable, in ways that might provide you with a way forward in your relationship with each other.

Barry: Okay, so how are we going to do that? Where do we start?

M: I have heard some things that have given me some ideas about where to start. Pearce, would it be okay by you if I was to interview Barry first, with you in the listening position? Then, at our next meeting, we could shift this arrangement around?

Pearce: That's fine with me.

M: Is that okay with you, Barry?

Barry: Fine with me.

M: Alright, but before we proceed with this it is going to be important for me to interview Pearce in a way that will help him find another position in relation to you Barry. Pearce, I would like to ask you some questions about any experiences that you might have had in which you felt strongly acknowledged by someone, or profoundly heard, or significantly accepted – about anything like this. And in this, I would appreciate it if you would exclude experiences of acknowledgement and acceptance from Barry, as it raises extra complications if you are positioned as Barry as you are listening to my conversation with Barry.

Pearce: Okay. But I am not sure about what you are asking me to talk about. You could maybe ask me some questions.

M: Alright. Could you think of a time when ....

In response to my questions, Pearce chose to speak of his 'coming out' story. He was nineteen years of age, and the double life that he had been living had become impossible for him to sustain any longer; he felt that he was breaking under the pressure of this double life, totally anguished over the contradictions in his existence, and now desperate to bring the worlds of his existence together. And yet Pearce was also anguished about this prospect of bringing these worlds together, and didn't know where to start in his efforts to achieve this. He loved the members of his family dearly, but found himself 'rocked' by their occasional expressions of homophobia, and constantly confronted by their heterosexist assumptions that were expressed in a 'thousand' ways in his every contact with them ('Who are you dating? At least tell us her name'). He just knew that he wasn't up to handling their immediate responses to the news that he was gay, or to educating them about the multiplicity of ways that their taken-for-granted assumptions about life and about his identity rendered him invisible.

Not knowing what else to do at this point of personal crisis, Pearce turned to his Uncle David, his mother's brother. Pearce'd had little contact with this uncle in recent years, but had many fond memories of the visits of this uncle when he was a small boy. At that time, Uncle David regularly visited Pearce's mother, and on these occasions would always bring Pearce a chocolate, and would always take time out to play cricket or football with him. Pearce called this uncle and told him that he urgently needed his help, and that he hadn't known who else he could turn to. Uncle David was immediately responsive, saying that he would cancel his golf on Saturday so that they could meet. However, it was a Thursday morning, and Pearce said that he just couldn't wait until Saturday. His uncle responded by cancelling his work appointments for that Thursday afternoon.

When Pearce sat down in his uncle's office, the 'flood gates opened'. He just 'blurted' everything out. He couldn't stop himself. He just 'talked at' his uncle non-stop for over an hour. What was his uncle's response? At the end of this time he simply stood up. Pearce's heart was in his mouth. He then went to Pearce, lifted him up, and held him firmly in his embrace. Pearce felt himself going limp in his uncle's arms, and then he began to 'cry, and cry, and cry yet more the tears of many years'. When Pearce was 'all cried out', he stepped back to see that his uncle's clothes were saturated through with his tears. But his uncle appeared not to notice. Instead his uncle talked about how incredibly touched he'd been by Pearce's story, and about how honoured he'd felt in being the family member chosen by Pearce to share this story of his life. Further, this uncle said that, if it was okay by Pearce, he could pave the way for Pearce's coming out to his family. He asserted that the responsibility of handling the preliminary responses of his family members shouldn't be on Pearce's shoulders, and that this was something he could assist them with. He also suggested that he follow this up with some conversations that might help them to become more aware of their many implicit assumptions that were disqualifying of Pearce's life and rendering his identity invisible. This triggered off a new round of crying – in regard to this, Pearce said 'Again I just couldn't help myself, and was so glad that I didn't have to' – and by the time he met with the members of his family they'd had the opportunity to 'process their reactions with Uncle David' and had prepared an apology for the ways that they had all played a part in his marginalisation.

Upon hearing this story I talked with Pearce about how moving I'd found it. Barry joined in this with: 'I have heard this story before, but I still find it very moving. I wish I'd had an uncle like this, as it would have made it much easier for me.' I then began to interview Pearce about this story in ways that I hoped would be distilling of his uncle's practices of acknowledgement as an expression of specific skills and of certain sentiments of living. It was my understanding that this distillation would assist Pearce to reposition himself for my interview with Barry. This interview featured questions like:

- *Of the words that your uncle used, which did you find particularly acknowledging?*
- *What was the tone of his voice when he was speaking these words?*
- *Which of his movements – whether they be of his gestures, his facial expressions, his posture, his demonstrative actions, the rhythm of his breath, or whatever – were particularly congruent with these words and this tone of voice?*
- *What was it about the timing of your uncle's expressions that was so validating of you?*
- *What values were expressed in these words, in this tone, in these movements, and in this timing?*
- *In his responses he was very attuned to what was important to you, and to what would encourage you to speak of what you hadn't spoken. What do these responses suggest about how he oriented himself to your life? What do these responses suggest about what he had high regard for in the story of your life?*
- *What was it about his responses that conveyed such a strong sense of understanding?*
- *What was it about his responses that provided you with a sense of how touched he'd felt by your story, and by the fact that you had chosen him to speak to at this critical time of your life?*
- *What did his responses suggest about what he wanted for you, and about what he hoped for as an outcome of your meeting with him?*

Having attended to these preparations for Pearce's repositioning, I inquired about his readiness for the task to follow.[2]

M: Pearce, do you think that it would now be possible for you to assume a position of uncle-hood as you listen to the conversation that I am about to have with Barry?

Pearce: Sure. I could give it a go. Just spell it out a bit more for me.

M: Okay. The idea is that you will be endeavouring to listen to my conversation with Barry in the way that you imagine your Uncle David might be listening if he could be here. It's an idea about you making efforts to be here in the ways that you have been describing – with Uncle David's skills of acknowledging and affirming others available to you. And with the sort of values and beliefs that would be guiding him in this. This would require you to step back from your position as Barry's partner for the duration of our conversation, and it is my guess that it would make it possible for you to hear what you wouldn't otherwise hear, and to respond in ways that you might not otherwise be able to respond. And I believe that this could make it possible for you to achieve some things in your relationship with Barry that might not be possible for you to achieve at this present time from a Pearce position in relation to Barry.

Pearce: Alright. I think I could give this a go. I'm prepared to have a try at least.

M: What do you think Barry?

Barry: I like the idea, but I am not sure that Pearce will be able to do it. He too easily gets caught up in …

Pearce: There he goes again. For the life of me, I just don't get it. You always …

M: Barry, do you think that was entirely helpful?

Barry: Okay, okay, okay. I'll try to be good.

Pearce: Look, it's like I said before Michael, he really just can't help himself, and …

M: Uncle-hood!!

Pearce: Okay, okay.

M: If you do have a sense that it is getting too difficult for you to maintain this position, give me some sort of signal, and I'll take time out from my conversation with Barry and talk with you about whether it is a good idea to proceed with the exercise, and if so, about what would make it easier for you to be present in Uncle David ways.

Pearce: That's good. That's good.

M: Alright. Now Barry, I would like to pick up on what you were saying earlier about how some things that were acceptable to you in your relationship with Pearce are no longer acceptable.

Pearce: This is alright for Barry to say, but I am in this relationship too. Do you think this is just up to Barry to independently decide? I mean to decide what's acceptable and what's not in our relationship?

Barry: See Michael, I told you that he wouldn't be able to …

M: Barry, I can attend to this. This is my job. Pearce, you are presently responding to Barry from your position within this relationship. Should we take time out or …

Pearce: No, no. I'll concentrate. I want to do it. I can do it.

M: Okay. Barry, I would like to ask you some questions about this development, about how some things that were acceptable to you are no longer so. And Pearce will be listening as his Uncle David might be listening if he was present. Is that right Pearce?

Pearce: Yeah. That's what I am doing. That's what I am doing.

M: Barry, the fact that there were some things about the relationship that were acceptable to you that are now no longer acceptable suggests to me that you have had some new realisations that have clarified for you how you want to live your life. Or that perhaps that you are valuing yourself in ways that you weren't previously. Or that there have been some developments in your sense of personal worth. Or something like this.

Barry: Well, I've not really thought about this. But yeah, I think I am clearer about how I want things to be in our relationship. And yeah, I guess it's true that this is about the fact that I am valuing myself more.

M: Valuing yourself in what sort of terms? Valuing what about yourself?

Barry: Well, just being more aware of some of my talents I guess. It's about my ability to be creative, to make things up as I go along, to find other ways of getting done what I want to get done. You know, getting away from the same old routines. Yeah. That's it. I'm clearer about the fact that it doesn't suit me anymore to stick to lots of routines that I find just so boring, or to accept situations where I am just expected to step aside from what works for me.

M: It is my guess that these realisations didn't come out of the blue. Is there anything that you could tell me about recent developments in your life that could have contributed to these realisations. I'm thinking of the sort of developments that might have helped you to value yourself more and that might have clarified for you how you want to live your life?

Barry: Hmm …The main one I think would be my enrolment in Art School.

M: Would you mind telling me about that?

Barry: It was about eight months ago. I started going to Art School. This is something that I had wanted to do for many years, but I never thought I would be up to it. I didn't think that I'd have the talent. In the end I took a chance on it, and had a pact with myself that I would pull out if it wasn't working out after six weeks.

M: What happened?

Barry: My work was pretty scrappy, but two of my teachers took an interest in it. I don't know how they saw what they did in my work, and I wasn't convinced at the beginning, but over several weeks I began to get the idea that they were onto something, that they weren't just making it up to make me feel better. I began to get the idea that I might have a bit of artistic talent. This was fantastic for me to see, and I was on such a high then. This was a high that I couldn't have imagined. Anything I had imagined wouldn't have come close to this. If it hadn't been for Sarah and Roger's (two of Barry's art teachers) encouragement and support, I'd be out of there now. But things just seem to get better in this part of my life.

M: What's your sense of what was reflected about you in your early artistic efforts? In looking at your work back then, what's your guess about what your art teachers caught a glimpse of? And I'd be interested in your thoughts about what this told them about your talents, or about how you see life, or about what is important to you.

Barry: I actually know some of the answers to these questions, particularly because Sarah is a very direct person, and doesn't hold things back. What she said was …

This account of recent developments in Barry's life unfolded further in the context of this re-authoring conversation. Over this time, Pearce only had difficulty in maintaining an uncle-hood position on two occasions, which seemed a significant achievement in view of the intensity of this couple's conflict at the outset of the interview. It was now time for the outsider-witness retelling. I invited Barry to sit back and listen to me interview Pearce about what he had heard. This interview was structured around the four categories of inquiry that I have discussed in this paper.

M: At this point the plan is for Barry to sit back and be an audience to my conversation with you, Pearce. I won't be asking you for your opinions, or to give advice, or to make any judgements, but will be interviewing you according to a scheme that I have found to be very helpful in these circumstances. It is my responsibility to keep things on course, so, if it is okay with you, I'll increase the tempo of my questions if I sense that this is important. Is this okay with you?

Pearce: Yeah. That's fine. I'd rather you have this responsibility than me have it.

M: Okay. Let's get going. From an uncle-hood position, as you were listening to Barry's story, what did you hear that most caught your attention Pearce?

Pearce: To be honest, at first it was difficult to hear lots of the things that Barry was saying. I'd be falling back into our relationship thing, and feeling indignant, and all sorts of other things. But after a while I found that I could imagine what my Uncle David might be hearing, about what would have interested him, and it did get a whole lot easier.

M: What was it in Barry's story that you were drawn to when you stepped into this uncle-hood position?

Pearce: Actually it was lots of things. But what stood out most was the joy that Barry had when his art teachers confirmed the fact that he had some artistic ability.

M: Do you recall the words that Barry used when he talked about what this was like for him?

Pearce: Yeah. He said that he hadn't imagined anything that could have even come close to this. But it wasn't just this. It was also what he said about this connection that he has with Sarah. That it's honest and that it is supportive and encouraging.

M: You said that you were drawn to lots of things from the position of uncle-hood.

Pearce: Yeah. There were all those things that Barry said about what he had realised about his life. It was about the clarity that he's now got about how he wants his life to be. I am sure that my Uncle David would pick up on this.

M: I am always interested to know what catches people's attention when they are in the listening position and when they are free to hear what they might not otherwise hear. And I am also interested to know about what this sets off in people's minds, about the images that come to them about the person's life, the mental pictures that come to mind at these times. What is your guess about the sort of images that would have come to your uncle's mind had he been present? And how do you think he would speak about these images?

Pearce: What images came to mind about Barry's life?

M: Yes. About what images were evoked by Barry's story. Take what you were drawn to in Barry's story when you were standing in your uncle's shoes. In this position, how did this affect your picture of Barry as a person, or your sense of what his life is about?

Pearce: Yeah. Actually, I do think that I was able to stand in my uncle's shoes for some of this. And I did have a lot of images. Some of these had to do with picturing Barry arriving at some place where he is valuing himself in a different way. At a position in life where some things are falling into place more for him. Yeah. I would say at a place where there is more harmony between his life and how he wants it to be. And the image of his connection with Sarah was very much there as well.

M: You have talked about what you were drawn to in Barry's story from an uncle-hood position, and about some of the images that this set off for you. Do you have any sense of what these words touched on for you? For example, did they strike a chord with something in your own life, with experiences of your own personal history?[3]

Pearce: This is not about uncle-hood?

M: No, it is about Pearce. I am now asking you to be Pearce again, and if it gets too difficult to stay with this development, I could again interview you as Uncle David.

Pearce: Okay. What did it touch on for Pearce? Yeah. I'm a bit confused about this. Maybe it is jealousy that I am feeling. Barry is finding more harmony in his life, and he has these wonderful connections with his art teachers, and I think that maybe I am just jealous about this.

M: Do you feel jealous right now?

Pearce: No. Not really. I just don't know how to say it. It is something, but right now I don't actually feel at all jealous.

M: Well how would you describe what Barry's story is touching on for you right now? Would you say it is a desire, or a wish, or a longing, or a …

Pearce: A longing! That's it! That's the word I was looking for. There were things that Barry said about developments in his life that I think touched on a longing in my life.

M: Do you speak of this longing often?

Pearce: Actually, you won't believe this, but I've never talked about this before. It is the sort of longing to arrive at the sort of place that Barry is arriving at in his life. Art isn't at all my thing, but I think I have longed for the sort of connection that Barry has with his art teachers.

M: Has this longing been with you for some time?

Pearce: Yeah. Now that I think about it, it's been since I can remember.

M: I'd like to ask you a question about this experience. You have listened to this story about recent developments in Barry's life, and you have been responding to what you heard in Barry's story from an uncle-hood position. And you have also been responding from a Pearce position. Would you say a little about where all of this has taken you?

Pearce: Do you mean right now?

M: Yeah. What place are you in now in your thoughts or understanding or feelings or perceptions or whatever, that you would not be in if you hadn't been present as an audience to Barry's story, and if you hadn't had this opportunity to respond to Barry's story?

Pearce: Well, I certainly wouldn't be speaking about this longing, that's for sure. And this is something different.

M: What's it like for you to be openly acknowledging this longing?

Pearce: Well, in some ways I am in a bit of a painful place right now. Getting in touch with these longings in this way hurts a bit. I don't know where to go with this right now.

M: Do you regret this? Getting in touch with these longings in this way, I mean, because this is painful.

Pearce: No. No. This is the first time that I have openly spoken about these longings, and I reckon that this has to be a step forward. This has to be a step in the right direction. And who knows, maybe it will encourage me to take a leaf out of Barry's book. You know, in a way that I will be following up on some of these longings.

M: Okay. It is probably time that we switched things around again. Would it now be okay for you to sit back so that I can interview Barry about what he heard in your retelling of his story?

Pearce: Yeah. It's a good time.

M: Okay. Barry, what did you hear in Pearce's retelling that caught your attention?

Barry: (tearful) Phew! It was all a bit overwhelming really. Where do I start? Phew! How Pearce acknowledged the joy that I was finding in my art work and, let's see, yeah, about my connection with my teachers and about what he said about the harmony that this is bringing to my life. And, yeah, about the longings this touched on in Pearce's life. Everything really! And it wasn't just what Pearce said you know, but it was also what was in his voice. From this I got the sense that he really was happy about what's happening in my life. I never thought that I would hear this from Pearce, I really didn't. Phew!

M: So many things! Earlier I asked Pearce about the mental pictures that your story set off for him. Did Pearce's retelling evoke further images of your own life, or of who you are? Did it contribute to any further realisations about your life?

Barry: Yeah. Somehow it made everything more vivid, even more real. I think it somehow made these realisations I've been having even stronger realisations.

M: Would you like to say something about these realisations?

Barry: There is so much to say about them, and I need more time to think about these. I will say that I'm seeing myself as a person who is more connected to what it is important for me to be connected to, to the things that are special to me. And this had me thinking a lot about my mother. She was a single parent. We didn't have very much, but she always let me know that I was special to her. I was always special to her. And she always let me know that it was just fine for me to be who I was.

M: You have talked about what you heard from Pearce that stood out for you, and about the images of your life that this evoked. Do you have a sense of what this struck a chord with in your own personal history, that resonated for you in this?

Barry: That's easy to answer. As a little boy I used to dream about my life, about my future. Lots of wonderful scenarios. I remember not wanting to wake from these beautiful dreams. But I lost touch with these dreams when I became an adolescent, and after that felt terribly lonely and desperate. At the time I was just plain bewildered about this, and about virtually everything that was happening around me. Later I could look back and see what happened. I now realise that I ran headfirst into all of this bigotry, and all of this homophobia. I nearly lost my life to it. Literally, I nearly did. I came close to killing myself many times. It was like I hit this brick wall. It was like a knock-out blow. These dreams, well they got knocked out of my life. Anyway, it's a long answer to your questions, but I would say that as I listened to Pearce I felt some of these dreams stirring again (tearful).

M: One last question before we wind up this conversation. Earlier I asked Pearce where this conversation had taken him. I will ask you the same question.

Barry: You know, it's strange, but I feel that I have come a long way in this. To feel reconnected with mum. And these dreams, to feel them stirring. This is somewhere else, it really is. There is a lot to talk about in all of this. I don't know where it has got me to in my connection with Pearce, but his words have played a big part in this.

This was the first of eight meetings with Pearce and Barry. They went away knowing that at the next meeting Pearce would occupy the centre of the definitional ceremony. Barry had thought ahead about who he might be repositioned as, and he chose Sarah, one of the art teachers who had been so supportive of him. He attended this meeting in drag, wearing some of his 'dress ups' and some items of clothing that Sarah had lent him. Barry had talked with Sarah about the events of our first meeting and had shared his wish to reposition himself as her in the next meeting. Sarah had said that she'd felt honoured by this, and thought that some items of her own clothing might contribute to the occasion. As Sarah, Barry's retelling of Pearce's story was quite phenomenal.

What was the subject for the starting-point for my interview with Pearce? It was the longings that he had voiced from the outsider-witness position in our first meeting. I began this interview with some questions that I hoped would assist Pearce to draw out the history of these longings. Since these were longings that he had maintained a connection with through these years, some of these questions were directed to the identification of experiences that may have verified the relevance of these longings to his life. In response to these questions, Pearce began to talk about his father. He was a man who wasn't physically demonstrative, who worked around the clock seven days a week in his work as an accountant, and whose life seemed devoid of longings. However, as Pearce had spoken of his father in response to my questions about the history of these longings in his life, I thought that it would be worthwhile to ask a few more questions about their relationship. I specifically asked Pearce about experiences of his father that might have been validating of such longings. It was then that Pearce recalled his high school graduation. His father had been present for this, and this was one of those rare occasions upon which this man had been demonstrative. After the graduation ceremony, his father had briefly embraced him, and had said, with tears in his eyes: 'Don't do it like I did it son'. He then turned, and was gone.

This account of this father's response to Pearce's high school graduation many years ago provided the point of entry to a re-authoring conversation that was richly describing of Pearce's life and identity. In this conversation there was some speculation about what it would be like for Pearce's father to be present, and to hear about the steps that Pearce was now taking to acknowledge these longings, steps that his father hadn't had the opportunity to take. This was also a deeply moving interview, and, as I said, Barry's retelling of Pearce's story was phenomenal – but that is another story.

At Pearce and Barry's invitation, Uncle David and Sarah joined our fifth meeting and were positioned as outsider-witnesses as Pearce and Barry talked of developments in their personal lives and in their relationship. These were developments that were very satisfying to both of them. In regard to their relationship, Pearce and Barry were now more at ease with each other; they reported on spontaneous developments in give and take, on a very significant reduction in conflict, and on the growth of fun times together. They were still having some disagreements, but in the context of these they were finding that they could now acknowledge each other's position on the subject of the dispute. Pearce and Barry also talked about the ways in which Uncle David and Sarah's sentiments of living had contributed to these developments. When it was Uncle David and Sarah's turn to speak, amongst other things, they talked about how honoured they felt at being included in Pearce and Barry's relationship in the way that they were.

At the end of our series of meetings, and at follow up, it was clear that the last vestiges of the chronic conflict which had become a central feature of Barry and Pearce's relationship had dissolved. I use the term dissolved, as at no time in our work was the focus on conflict resolution. I certainly didn't assist in the negotiation of any conflicts or act as a mediator in any of our contacts. Rather than conflict resolution, the approach that I have described here contributes to conflict dissolution. This is conflict dissolution that is achieved through: the rich story development of the lives of partners of couple relationships; the interruption of efforts to resolve difficulties through recourse to culturally venerated communicational processes; the erosion of exclusivity in couple relationships; and through the adoption of other relational forms in ways that contributes to diversity of response in couple relationships – in this instance Pearce and Barry incorporated the uncle/nephew, mentor/student and colleague/colleague (on some levels, Barry's relationship with his art teachers was collegial) relational forms.

Conclusion

In this paper I have proposed that the difficulties experienced by couples in high and longstanding conflict and the difficulties often experienced by therapists in their consultations with these couples have a common genesis. This genesis is to be found in assumptions that privilege a style of communication that came to be cherished in the post-World War Two era of information technology, and in the further development of expectations for exclusivity in couple relationships in contemporary western culture. I then introduced an approach to working with couples in high and longstanding conflict that is founded on narrative practices of 'definitional ceremony' and the 'repositioning' of the outsider witness. Amongst other things, this approach displaces this cherished communicational style, and contributes to a suspension of this exclusivity of the modern couple relationship.

I have consistently found this approach effective in achieving conflict dissolution with couples in high and longstanding conflict. I have also found that this approach has a relevance beyond conflict dissolution. Over the last several years I have been employing this approach more routinely in my work not just with couples with high and longstanding conflict, but with couples that have presented a broad range of difficulties for therapy. In this time, this approach has been equally effective in the dissolution of many of the other difficulties commonly experienced in couple relationships.

Notes

1. Many feminist scholars, for example, O'Brien (1981) and McNay (1992), have linked the development of this phenomenon to the privatisation of marriage and the family in the interests of patriarchy.
2. Fortunately I had managed to find an extended time slot for this first visit, and was able to take the next step of interviewing Barry with Pearce positioned as the outsider witness. However, I don't always have this luxury of time, and there have been occasions upon which this next step has been postponed until the next meeting.
3. On account of the richness of Pearce's retelling, at this juncture I thought it appropriate to risk inviting him to 'embody' his interest in Barry's expressions as Pearce, not as Uncle David. If it had turned out that Pearce was not ready for this, I knew that it would be relatively easy for me to assist him to again reposition himself

as Uncle David, and to encourage him to speculate about what aspects of Uncle David's personal experiences might have resonated with Barry's expressions, and about the ways in which these expressions might have moved Uncle David had he been present.

References

Foucault, M. 1994: 'The social triumph of the sexual will.' In Rabinow, P. (ed): *Michel Foucault: Ethics.* New York: Allen Lane – The Penguin Press.

Levenson, E.A. 1972: *The Fallacy of Understanding.* New York: Basic Books.

O'Brien, M. 1981: *The Politics of Reproduction.* London: Routledge & Kegan Paul.

McNay, L. 1992: *Foucault & Feminism: Power, gender and the self.* Cambridge: Polity Press.

Myerhoff, B. 1982: 'Life history among the elderly: Performance, visibility and re-membering.' In J. Ruby (ed): *A Crack in the Mirror: Reflexive perspectives in anthropology.* Philadelphia: University of Pennsylvania Press.

Myerhoff, B. 1986: 'Life not death in Venice: Its second life.' In Turner, V. & Bruner, E. (eds): *The Anthropology of Experience.* Chicago: University of Illinois Press.

White, M. 1995: 'Reflecting teamwork as definitional ceremony.' In White, M.: *Re-Authoring Lives: Interviews and essays.* Adelaide: Dulwich Centre Publications.

White, M. 1997: 'Definitional ceremony.' In White, M.: *Narratives of Therapists' Lives.* Adelaide: Dulwich Centre Publications.

White, M. 1999: 'Reflecting teamwork as definitional ceremony revisited.' *Gecko: A journal of deconstruction and narrative ideas in therapeutic practice*: #1. Reprinted in White, M. 2000: *Reflections on Narrative Practice: Essays and interviews.* Adelaide: Dulwich Centre Publications.

chapter two

Journey metaphors

Introduction

In this paper, I document the use of katharsis and rite of passage metaphors within therapy, teaching and community work contexts. This paper was written to be given as an evening address to participants prior to the Dulwich Centre Publications' International Narrative Therapy and Community Work Conference held at Spelman College in Atlanta in June, 2002. As practitioners from many different countries gathered together in the beautiful grounds of the historically black women's college, there was an increasing sense of anticipation about what experiences lay ahead of us. Never before had such an event been held at an historically black college, and participants and organisers alike felt powerfully welcomed by Vanessa McAdams-Mahmoud of Spelman College and the local African American community. We didn't know exactly where this was all leading, we only knew that we were delighted to be travelling together. What was clear was that thorough preparation would be required to make this event all that it could be. The writing and delivery of this paper was one aspect of these conference preparations. Now, almost two years later, we would once again like to thank Vanessa McAdams-Mahmoud, Vanessa Jackson and Makungu Akinyela for inviting us to host the conference at Spelman College, and for making possible what was a rigorous, generous-hearted and healing event.

Therapeutic journeys

Today, as much as ever, ahead of my first meetings with the people who consult me, I experience feelings of anticipation, degrees of apprehension, and a sense of heightened expectations. This is anticipation of other journeys to be had – not just any old journeys, but ones that will, like those before it, take me to destinations that I could not have predicted, by routes not previously mapped. This is an apprehension that relates to the responsibility that I have, as a therapist, for the travelling circumstances, and for the journey's outcome. And these are heightened expectations in regard to yet more opportunities to be transported to other places in life in which I might become other than who I was at the outset of the journey – amongst other things, expectations of opportunities to:

a) think beyond what I routinely think,
b) extend upon and to reconsider established understandings of my life and my identity,
c) engage anew with previously neglected aspects of my experience of life,
d) question what I take for granted and to have my settled certainties shaken up,
e) further develop the skills of therapeutic practice,
f) explore yet more considerations of personal, relationship, and community ethics.

To be sure, on account of this potential for these meetings to take me to unscheduled destinations via routes previously uncharted, my meetings with people who consult me over a wide range of predicaments, concerns and problems have always been significant personal and professional life-shaping encounters. And more than this, the people who have consulted me over the years have not only opened their lives to me in ways that, in the usual course of their lives, they do not to others, but they have also significantly included me in their lives. This inclusion is such that these people populate many of the territories of my identity – I regard them to be fellow travellers, and they have made a significant contribution to the cast of the characters of my life.

As I pause to reflect on this cast of characters drawn from my meetings with people over many years, so many stories flood into my memory. At this moment I am recalling a rascal of a boy named Harold*, who, when I was

---

* All names are pseudonyms.

working at the Adelaide Children's Hospital in the 1970s, after witnessing me riding my bicycle to work, bestowed on me the name 'Michael the cycle'. He quickly encouraged other children to follow suit, and this got around the hospital like wildfire. Suddenly, in the wards and the corridors, everywhere there were echoes of 'Michael the cycle'. In these echoes I experienced a sense of being held in a warm embrace by Harold and by many other children who were at the time inpatients of this hospital. I recall reflecting on this at the time, and became more strongly aware of how this and many developments like it built for me a sense of home in that hospital – in the sort of place where that sense of home is usually so elusive and difficult to establish.

Harold's 'Michael the cycle' also contributed to a wider acceptance of my informal ways in what was, in that era, a domain of high formality. I will always remember the occasion upon which a senior administrator for the first time summoned me with 'Michael the cycle'. Surprised by this slip, she quickly admonished herself, and began to apologise profusely. She then stopped – there was an awkward silence – and suddenly we were both laughing heartily. From that time forward I was to her 'Michael the cycle'.

Teaching journeys

The journey metaphor is not just relevant to my experience of working with families. I have also found it apt in regard to my experiences of teaching, particularly with regard to the more extended teaching assignments in smaller group contexts. These teaching experiences have also set me on journeys that have provided me with the opportunity to become other than who I was at the outset of these events. Apart from other things, it is in the context of these journeys that I have been able to develop ever more rich descriptions of my understandings of what goes in the name of narrative therapy, and to acquire a clearer appreciation of the relevant skills of narrative practice.

As I am reflecting on this I am thinking about the inspiration that I draw from so many therapists who have visited Dulwich Centre over the years, and the many others with whom I have had the opportunity to meet in faraway places. I have also felt your embrace, and have been nourished in the linking of the stories of our lives and our work around shared themes and values that are precious to us. Amongst other things, this has made it possible for me to carry on in contexts that would have otherwise discouraged me.

Community journeys

The journey metaphor has also been appropriate to my work with communities. Since the mid-nineties, we at Dulwich Centre have been invited to join with a number of communities in their efforts to address a range of pressing predicaments and concerns. In working with these communities I have been transported to other places I could not have imagined. For example, I have witnessed powerful expressions of the insider experiences of the people of these communities that have taken me into territories of knowledge that I could not have known.

Community members have supported and encouraged my forays into territories of awareness that I would not have otherwise had access to: territories of awareness that, amongst other things, feature a special consciousness of the power relations of local culture that are usually unquestioned and so often rendered invisible. This has also taken me into orbits of my familiar world from which it has been rendered newly strange and exotic. This has had the effect of deconstructing many of my assumptions about life and the world, and has introduced me to new perspectives on my own culture and ethnicity and to domains of personal experience that would not have otherwise been opened to me.

And, as in my work with families and in the context of my teaching assignments, I have found an extraordinary sense of inclusion in this work with communities, one that has touched my life in ways that I often find difficult to account for.

Meaning

In fact, on many occasions I find myself struggling to find appropriate words for the naming of the many ways that these conversations with individuals, couples, families, groups and communities touch my life and move me. To find words that endow these experiences with meanings that satisfactorily portray them to me and to others is a task not always easily accomplished. Often some of these words only come to me through the reflection of hindsight, and in conversations with others with whom I work. I have always believed this naming to be important, because how we think of these experiences of our work, how we accord these experiences meaning, contributes very significantly to how we receive them, to how we take them in, and to how we respond to them. The attribution of meaning to these movements of our lives is, I believe, a significant and important responsibility.

This emphasis on the acknowledgement of movement, and this attention to the attribution of meaning, is, in my mind, linked to the poststructuralist sentiment that is associated with narrative practice. Put briefly, according to this sentiment, all expressions of life are units of meaning and experience, and it is these expressions of life that significantly constitute our lives – it is these expressions that actually make our lives up. This sentiment draws our attention to the significance of the meanings that we attribute to our experiences of our conversations with the people who seek our help, and to the significance of the ways that we shape our expressions of these experiences. It draws our attention to the responsibility that we have, as therapists and community workers, for the meanings that we accord to our experiences of our work, and to the responsibility that we have for the ways in which we give expression to these meanings.

It is in embracing this responsibility that we have the opportunity to more fully recognise the potential of our therapeutic conversations to contribute to us being other than who we were at the outset of these conversations. And it turns out that the responsibility that we have for the making of meaning becomes a significant ethical responsibility, for it powerfully shapes the self- and relationship-forming activities that we engage in under the name of therapeutic practice.

However, having stated this, I want to acknowledge the extent to which engaging with this poststructuralist sentiment can be quite an achievement in our contemporary world. This is an achievement that is often hard-won as this sentiment runs against another sentiment that is popular, and that is tied to a different ethic, one that has become very much associated with modern liberal-humanist thought. In the context of this popular sentiment, therapeutic conversations are guided by the knowledges of life and identity that are possessed by the therapist ahead of the therapeutic encounter. These are knowledges of life and identity that are invariably informed by a modern rationality that is represented in the 'laws of human nature'. According to this scheme, the therapeutic context provides an opportunity for the people who consult therapists to become not other than who they are, but to become 'more truly who they really are' – to gain access to a life that is a more accurate expression of what it is that is considered to be 'human nature'. According to this sentiment, the therapist is a vehicle for these knowledges of life and identity, and, when all goes to plan, s/he is unchanged by the therapeutic encounter.

Because poststructuralist understandings run counter to this popular sentiment that evokes human nature, engaging with these understandings can be a significantly difficult task in this contemporary world. On account of this it can be helpful for us to take recourse to the sort of frames for meaning-making that provide fertile conditions for us to acknowledge the ways in which these conversations have made it possible for us to become other than who we were. There are many such frames that can assist us in making meaning that is acknowledging of the movement or the potential movement that we experience in these conversations. I will discuss two of these here. Both fit with the journey metaphor that I have been employing in this presentation.

Katharsis

The first of these is the katharsis metaphor. Here, I am not referring to a contemporary version of 'catharsis' that is associated with notions of discharge and release, but to 'katharsis' in what I understand to be a central classical understanding of this idea. This is a katharsis that was had in response to witnessing powerful expressions of life's dramas, and was particularly associated with one's response to the performance of Greek tragedy. I believe that katharsis, according to this definition, is an appropriate metaphor through which to attribute meaning to our own responses to the everyday dramas of life that we witness in our therapeutic conversations, in teaching contexts, and in working with communities.

According to this classical definition, an experience is kathartic if one is moved by it – moved not just in terms of having an emotional experience, but in terms of being transported to another place from which one might, amongst other developments:

a) have a new perspective on one's life and history and identity,
b) re-engage with neglected aspects of one's own history,
c) make new meanings of experiences not previously understood,
d) initiate steps in one's life otherwise never considered,
e) think beyond what one routinely thinks, and so on.

In taking our experiences of our work into this katharsis metaphor, our attention goes to what it is that we are most powerfully relating to in people's expressions of their experiences of life:

a) to what it is that strikes a chord for us,
b) to what it is that we are drawn to,
c) to what it is that most captures our imagination,
d) to what it is that fires our curiosity, and
e) to what it is that provokes our fascination.

This attention to what we are most powerfully relating to in people's expressions is usually accompanied by a heightening of awareness of our associative thoughts, and of the images of life and identity that are triggered by these expressions. These are images of life and identity that are often rich in metaphor and simile, and which can set of reverberations into the history of our lives. Like sound waves, these reverberations set off resonances as they touch the surfaces of our experiences of life – oft-neglected aspects of our lived experience begin to resonate with the expressions of the people who are consulting us, and with the images of life and identity that have been triggered by these expressions.[1] These experiences light up and come into memory, and this precipitates a sense of our lives being joined with the lives of those who consult us around shared themes.

Further, it is in the context of this katharsis metaphor that it becomes possible for us to identify and to acknowledge movement in the sense of being transported. That is, it becomes possible for us to identify the places that our therapeutic conversations have taken us to that we could not have predicted. And it becomes possible for us to acknowledge that, on account of these powerful expressions of life, we have become other than who we would have otherwise been if we had not been present to witness these expressions.

This identification and acknowledgement of transport raises new possibilities in regard to the development of ethical practice. It sponsors explorations of how we might express this experience in ways that would:

a) render it visible to the people who consult us,

b) at the same time keep at the centre of our conversations the agenda and the lived experience of the people who consult us,

c) diminish the sort of marginalisation that people feel as an outcome of experiencing oneself as the 'other' within the therapeutic context,

d) contribute to the further development of ethical self- and relationship-forming activities in therapeutic practice.

Rites of passage

The rite of passage metaphor provides another frame that can assist us in a making meaning that is acknowledging of the movement or the potential movement that we experience in these conversations.

The rites of passage I am referring to are those that facilitate transitions in life, and are composed of three phases: the 'separation' phase, the 'liminal or betwixt and between' phase, and the 're-incorporation' phase (Turner 1969). The first phase is heralded by a separation from some aspect of the known and familiar, and from a specific status in life. In the context of this separation, one's settled certainties are shaken up – what was surely known and familiar is no longer so, and what was taken-for-granted can no longer be so. This separation can be precipitated by a range of circumstances, planned and unplanned, welcome and unwelcome.

This separation catapults people into the liminal phase of this passage, one often characterised by heightened expectations, periods of confusion, and degrees of disorientation. At times this gives rise to despair, and when this cannot be apprehended in the context of a progressive journey, it can be difficult for people to endure it. When this is the case, people usually express a growing desire to bring about a premature closure of the journey through efforts to recapture what was – to reinstate old certainties, and to resurrect the previously familiar and taken-for-granted realities of life. However, when this discomfort can be understood within the context of a progression through the liminal phase of a rite of passage, it becomes more possible to endure this discomfort and to keep travelling. This understanding of such discomfort brings acknowledgement of the fact that there is always some distance between the point of separation from the familiar and taken-for-granted, and the point of arrival at another location in which aspects of life and identity are experienced anew.

Then, at last, there is reincorporation, as one begins to derive a sense that one is arriving at another place in life, at new ground. This is new ground that can feature novel understandings of life and identity, a modified sense of self, a different appreciation of life, new sensibilities, and fresh proposals for directions in which one might proceed in life. Through inquiry, whatever it is that one has arrived at can become richly known and publicly acknowledged – at times this acknowledgement occurs in the context of ceremony. It is this public acknowledgement that significantly contributes to the endurance of the new.

Complexities

I have proposed that the katharsis and rite of passage metaphors can be of assistance in engaging with the poststructuralist sentiment. These metaphors provide frames that make it possible for us to:

a) attend to the responsibility that we have for the meanings that we accord to our experiences of our work, and for the expression that we give to these experiences,

b) acknowledge the potential of our therapeutic conversations to contribute to us being other than who we are at the outset of these conversations,

c) step into the ethical responsibility that we have in the shaping of the self- and relationship-forming activities of our therapeutic practice.

Apart from assisting us to engage with the poststructuralist sentiment, these frames are of assistance to us when we find that we are touched by our work in ways that unsettle, in ways that are initially difficult for us to find any comfort in. Experiences that have the potential to contribute to a sense of movement in our lives and work do not always go smoothly. These experiences are not always associated with a sense of new possibility, do not always bring a sense of heightened expectation, and are not always associated with pleasure. These experiences are not always, in the first place, welcomed. In fact, in this movement we can at times find ourselves being taken to places that are quite painful, and this can discourage meaning-making efforts that might be identifying of the transporting nature of our work.

For example, at times there will be occasions in our work upon which some of our taken-for-granted ideas and settled certainties about life are significantly confronted, and, as an outcome of this, we might find ourselves struggling with degrees of bewilderment, embarrassment, hurt, humiliation, disappointment, and general discomfort. On some of these occasions our immediate response will be to attempt premature closure of the journey by striving to reinstate our familiar and taken-for-granted 'truths' about life, and to reinvest in these. We can, in these responses, even find ourselves reproducing the very notions that contradict values and beliefs we hold dear. On such occasions we can wind up feeling very much out of sorts with ourselves.

At other times we will find conversations touching on painful memories, including those experiences of life that were disqualifying of and diminishing of us. On these occasions our immediate response can be to instigate efforts to bring about closure. There are many ways that this can be done, including through the development of negative interpretations of the motives of the people who are seeking our help. When we succeed in these efforts to bring about closure, what was potentially a new initiative in our lives becomes stalled.

Judy

In our supervision meeting, Judy chose to talk about what she was finding unsettling in her work with a newly referred family. Within the context of her conversations with this family, Judy had experienced what she described as a 'negative psychological reaction' that she found quite painful. She couldn't figure this out, as, in these conversations, she hadn't been aware of anything that she believed could account for this reaction. In her efforts to quickly resolve this, she had begun to manufacture some negative interpretations of the motives of the family members, but felt that in doing so she was compromising her values. In inviting Judy to take this experience into the meaning-making frame provided by the katharsis metaphor, I encouraged her to:

a) discern which of the family member's expressions she might be responding to,
b) describe the images of life and identity that could have been triggered by these expressions,
c) speculate about what it was in the history of her lived experience that might be resonating with this, and to
d) reflect on the ways in which this was potentially moving of her.

In endeavouring to define what it was that she was responding to, Judy became aware that she had been drawn to some significant expressions of acceptance of the daughter by the parents of this family. In describing the images that these expressions had evoked, and in tracing what it was from her own history that had resonated with these images, Judy became aware of how this had awakened a significantly contrasting experience – that is, it had awakened, in her, memories of the painful rejection that she had felt from her own parents. In responding to my inquiry about why this rejection was so painful to her, and about why this pain had arisen in the context of what she had witnessed in this family, Judy gave voice to a powerful 'longing for recognition and acceptance'. This was a longing for recognition and acceptance that she was not generally conscious of, and that she had rarely publicly acknowledged.

As this was a longing that Judy had continued to hold onto despite discouragement, I was curious about what experiences of life might have been sustaining of this longing. After some discussion, Judy began to recall her connection with the parents of one of her school friends. For a time these parents had included Judy in aspects of their family life in ways that she felt recognised and accepted. This came to a sudden end when Judy's family relocated to another part of town.

Judy assumed that it would be possible to discover the whereabouts of these parents of her school friend, and she was enthusiastic about the prospects of informing them of the significance of their act of inclusion of her as a young girl. She believed that this action would constitute a further expression of, and an open acknowledgement of, this longing, and that this would be transporting of her in significant ways. She also formulated a plan for acknowledging, in an appropriate fashion, to the members of the newly referred family, the ways in which her life had been touched by their expressions.[2]

I believe that explicit engagement with these metaphors of katharsis and rites of passage can provide a context that will be sustaining of us through these difficult experiences. Such explicit engagement with these metaphors contributes to:

a) the presence of mind that is required to render these painful experiences meaningful,

b) our capacity to endure what would otherwise be unendurable,

c) options for us to resist the desire to bring about a premature closure of the journey, and to

d) the further development or our ability to respond in ways that fit with the ethical responsibility that I have discussed in this paper.

This conference

This brings me to the subject of this conference. As in our meetings with families, groups, and communities, and as in teaching contexts, there is the potential for this conference to be transporting of us in ways that we could not have imagined. As an outcome of attending this conference there will be many possibilities for us to transported, to be moved in ways that we could not have expected, to become other than who we were at its outset. In the course of this, there will be experiences that will:

a) stretch our minds and our imagination,

b) invite us to think beyond what we would otherwise be thinking,

c) connect us with our own histories in new ways, and that will

d) raise possibilities for action in the world that would not have otherwise occurred to us.

Some of these experiences will include challenges to what is widely known and accepted about culture, race, class, heterosexism, gender, and sexual identity. Some of this will go smoothly, and will be a source of delight and celebration. But some will be difficult and unsettling of our familiar worlds.

These more difficult experiences are potentially fraught in the sense that they can contribute to a desire to bring about premature closure of the journey, and a reassertion of what is generally known. I say potentially fraught, as this is not inevitable. These experiences will only be fraught if we do not attend to the responsibility that we have for the making of meaning, and to the consequences of this in our expressions of life.

In regard to experiences of discomfort, I believe that for us to organise our experience around these metaphors of katharsis and rites of passage will make it possible for us to persist with our journeys in a way that we would not otherwise be able to persist. I believe that for us to organise our experience around these metaphors can render what is potentially fraught a source of inspiration in our lives and work.

In closing, I offer this paper as an invitation to us all to engage with the events of the coming days of this conference, and with each other, in ways that might contribute to:

a) a heightened awareness of the ways that we are becoming other than who we were at its outset,

b) the plotting of the courses of our journeys to destinations that we might not have predicted,

c) attention to the making of meaning in response to our experiences of the events of these days, and to how we are giving expression to these experiences within the context of this conference,

d) navigating transitions that might not always be comfortable to us,

e) a consciousness of the images of life and personal resonance that we are encountering in this event,

f) appropriate acknowledgement of the ways that this touches our lives, and of the places that this has taken us to.

Notes

1. Gaston Bachelard (1969) employs the terms 'reverberation' and 'resonance' in accounting for the inverse history of the images of reverie.

2. Judy did subsequently acknowledge this in the context of a meeting with this family. This act assisted family members to more deeply appreciate certain developments in their relationships with each other, including the headway made by the parents in accepting and appreciating their daughter's decisions about her own life, and the daughter's openness and responsiveness to this acceptance and appreciation. This experience of being joined in the acknowledgement of diversity contributed significantly to the resolution of the problems for which this family had sought therapy.

References

Bachelard, G. 1969: *The Poetics of Space*. Boston: Beacon Press.

Turner, V. 1969: *The Ritual Process.* New York: Cornell University Press.

chapter 3

Folk psychology and narrative practice

Introduction

In the first part of this paper I link many of the practices of narrative therapy to an historical tradition of understanding life and identity that is at times referred to as 'folk psychology'. This tradition, which was largely displaced by the modern psychologies, began to be reinstated when the social sciences went through an 'interpretive turn' in the late 1960s and early 1970s. I discuss the extent to which many of the practices of narrative inquiry can be located within the context of this interpretive turn, and within the tradition of folk psychology. In the second part of this paper I clarify some of the proposals for therapeutic practice that are shaped by this tradition of folk psychology. Finally, in the third part, I focus on considerations of history and culture, and on the implications of these considerations for therapeutic practice. To begin these explorations, I will describe a therapeutic conversation that I had with Paul, who consulted me about his work as a counsellor.

Part One

Folk psychology

Paul*

Paul consulted me about some concerns that he had about his work. He was a counsellor in a local agency, working mostly with heterosexual couples. Although there was much that he enjoyed about his work, in recent times he had become increasingly uncomfortable about some of his responses to the expressions of the male partners of these couple relationships. These were responses of anxiety and uncertainty, and Paul had reached the conclusion that this had to do with deep-seated fears and insecurities that were the outcome of his 'unresolved issues'. This spectre of unresolved issues weighed heavily on him, spinning him into uncertainty, and provoking dread. As well, the fact of the presence of these unresolved issues had Paul questioning his fitness to be working with people.

Paul: So that is where I am at with this fear thing. Sometimes it's more than fear. I'm shaking inside, virtually terrified. And I have been having a lot of questions about what I am doing in this work. I have even thought that maybe it is a sick thing. You know, that I am in this for the wrong reasons, that I have some weird motive. You know, for the motive of trying to work through the things that are unresolved, to do this for myself through my work. This has got to be pretty bad, you know.

M: Would you say a little more about this motive that …

Paul: Well, it's probably because I haven't sorted things out with my father, that I am, and this is without realising it too, that I am doing this through my work. Which I reckon is pretty screwed up.

M: You have had this idea for a while?

---

* All names are pseudonyms.

Paul: Yeah.

M: Has it helped a lot?

Paul: Nope. Not so far. In fact, not one little bit [laughs] But then, I don't know what the answer is.

M: Could we go back a step or two? Do you have a sense of what it is that you are responding to in these men when you feel this apprehension most? What it is that you are experiencing at the time in your conversations with these men? Do you have any thoughts about what it is that you witness, that contributes to this fear and anxiety?

Paul: Just little things really. Nothing much. It's pretty silly really. Sometimes I think it is just my imagination.

M: Like?

Paul: Like a look, hmm … or a way of sitting or, let me see … certain words or a tone of voice, and ... maybe a gesture. Like I said, just little things really. Lots of really silly little things can get me going, that can trigger it. You know, it's like ... it's like as if I am always on the alert.

M: On the alert? Tell me this. You said unresolved issues, and you mentioned your father, so I am making a guess. What would expressions like these have alerted you to at earlier times in your life?

Paul: Well … yeah, that's it. Of something brewing in my father, of a mood coming on ... Probably trouble, lots of trouble. Of manipulation too ... yeah, he was really into that. Yeah, there would be things that would have alerted me to danger.

M: Your mother too?

Paul: You mean, alerted me to danger from her?

M: No. I mean did she also have a sensitivity to these early-warning signs?

Paul: Yeah. I think we got together on this and helped each other out. We could see things coming.

M: And what sort of actions did you take in response to these early-warning signs, in response to these cues?

Paul: Well, we couldn't do much really. My mum could distract him sometimes. And so could I. You know, I always worried so much about my mum. When I think about it, I guess that knowing how to read these cues did help us to get out of harm's way at times. But, it wasn't enough … [trails off]

M: I take it that you and your mother validated this sense for each other. This sense that you had of the potential for harm. You joined with each other in developing this sensitivity to these cues. And you also supported each other in the limited actions that were available to you both.

Paul: We would work together on it. Yeah. But ... [tears welling, and chest heaving] … there I go again [brushing away the tears].

M: Would you mind saying a little about those tears?

Paul: It's okay. Just thinking about my mum you know, and about, well, what she went through and how hard she tried. And, and, about how unfair it was and about what she achieved despite all of this. And about our connection. Other things too.

M: What would she think about the work experiences that you are consulting me over? What is your guess about how she would be responding if she was present and hearing what I am hearing?

Paul: I think that she would feel for me a lot, and that she would be worried for me [now openly crying].

M: If I could ask her for her thoughts about why you had chosen to work in this area, what do you think she would say?

Paul: Well, she was mostly respectful of my decisions, not always though [now grinning through tears]. Sometimes she would get really mad at me. Maybe she'd say: 'Are you stark raving mad? What in the hell are you doing this to yourself for, after all that we went through?'

M: If she did see your choice of work as a significant decision, one not taken lightly, then what do you reckon she would say?

Paul: Yeah. Actually, I really think she would you know. She would probably say that it was because I wanted everyone to have a fair go. She would probably say that I knew what it was all about in lots of ways. She would probably under-stand that I just couldn't leave it.

M: So she might connect the fact of your working in this area with a purpose?

Paul: I reckon she would. She would probably say something about what I stood for, back then you know, although I wished that I'd been able to do more, I just … I do want everyone to have a fair go that's true, and no-one should have to live under a cloud like this.

M: Could it be that these are the sort of purposes that you and your mother's life were joined in?

Paul: For sure. For sure. But she never had a chance.

M: What do you reckon it would have been like for your mum to know that these purposes live on in your work in the way that they do?

Paul: [crying again] I reckon it would have meant heaps to her. Just heaps. And hey, the surprising thing is that I hadn't really thought much about this.

M: What is your guess about how she would feel about her own life, just knowing this?

Paul: [still crying] She wouldn't feel empty. She wouldn't feel that all the hard work had been for nothing.

As this conversation evolved further there was an opportunity to evoke the presence of Paul's mother (who was deceased). Later, the theme of sensitivity to cues returned to the centre of the conversation.

M: Picking up on this sensitivity to cues that you and your mother helped one another develop. Would you say that there was a skill in this?

Paul: Well, I have never really thought about that. Till now I have just seen it as a liability.

M: What would you say now?

Paul: Yeah. Now I would definitely say that.

M: Say what? That it is a skill?

Paul: Yeah. Although I haven't thought of it in this way before. Hey!

M: What?

Paul: I really like thinking about this.

M: Could I check something with you? I understand, from all that you have said, that the insecurities, fears and unresolved issues that you have talked of are, well, that they are part of a bundle of things. That these things speak of a sensitivity to certain cues about danger and potential for harm – of skills in reading these cues. That they speak of insider knowledges about the effects of intimidation and disrespect and abuse. That they speak about a valuing of and belief in other ways of being in life, of the sort that were reflected in your connection with your mother. And that they speak of a purpose that has been present through the history of your life, about contributing to everyone having a fair go, that you are joined with your mother in. I wanted to check this understanding out with you.

Paul: That's great! I can relate to all of that, and it feels so good [grinning again].

M: What is the good feeling? Could you say something about this?

Paul: Relief … relief … because this isn't all so bad is it, after all. I mean, I had been feeling like I was a fake counsellor with the insecurities and all of those unresolved issues. But this isn't so bad, is it? [now laughing]

M: I was thinking something similar. In fact I was thinking about what your work would look like if everything that has been bundled up in this anxiety and fear was more explicitly present in your work with the couples that are consulting you.

Paul: I can't imagine. But I would put myself up for a conversation about that.

The ensuing conversation centred on this exploration. In it, Paul determined that he could more explicitly take up, into his work, the sensitivity that he had to these cues, as well as these insider knowledges about the practices and consequences of intimidation and disrespect. He developed some specific ideas about how he might give expression to this sensitivity and to these knowledges, and about how this could open space for conversations about that which usually cannot be spoken of. In this conversation Paul also settled on some ideas about alternative avenues for the expression of what he had previously referred to as his insecurities. He practiced some of these ideas in the context of our meetings with me playing the part of the male partners of some of the couples that had been consulting him. For example, he would try out preludes to inquiries addressing practices of intimidation such as: 'Right now I would like to share with you the sort of questions that I would be asking you if it wasn't for my apprehension about how you might respond to them. I would appreciate it if you would reflect on these questions, and then tell me about whether or not this apprehension would be valid if I was to ask you these questions'.

Paul also thought of options for addressing the sort of circumstances that would make it difficult to proceed with these therapeutic conversations, and other options for openly negotiating the sort of circumstances that would make progress possible. I had two subsequent meetings with Paul, in which he caught me up with some really exciting developments in his work in addressing the power relations of gender with heterosexual couples. In one of these meetings he also informed me that he had found himself more able to provide an account of his work to friends in terms of his purposes without feeling embarrassed. He then joked that he longed for some more unresolved issues that we might turn upside down in our conversations with each other, and hoped that I would be able to detect a few of these. I suggested that he go down the street to get some of these, and bring them back with him next time. We both laughed.

Folk psychology

Many aspects of this account of my conversation with Paul are shaped by questions and reflections that are informed by what I refer to as narrative practices. Invariably I find that the people who consult me relate to these practices quite instantaneously, and this provides the basis for many wonderful adventures in the context of therapeutic conversations. I believe that the familiarity that people have with this sort of therapeutic inquiry has to do with the fact that many of the practices of narrative therapy are closely linked to a particular tradition of understanding life and identity that is deeply historical. At times this centuries old tradition is referred to as 'folk psychology' (Bruner 1990).

> *All cultures have as one of their most powerful constitutive instruments a folk psychology, a set of more or less connected, more or less normative descriptions about how human beings 'tick', what our own and other minds are like, what one can expect situated action to be like, what are possible modes of life, how one commits oneself to them, and so on. ... Coined in derision by the new cognitive scientists for its hospitality toward such intentional states as beliefs, desires, and meanings, the expression of 'folk psychology' could not be more appropriate ...* (pp. 35-36)

According to this definition, we routinely employ folk psychology as we make our way through everyday life. We put this folk psychology into service in our efforts to understand our own lives and in making sense of the actions of others. Folk psychology equips us with a range of notions about what makes people 'tick', and provides a foundation for our responses to the actions of others – our responses to the actions of others are premised on these understandings about what makes them tick, and by our conclusions about the nature of these actions. Folk psychology also comes to the fore in our efforts to make out just what it is that is going on in the world. Among other achievements, Bruner (1990) illustrates the way that folk psychology shapes our endeavour to come to terms with the unexpected in life, provides a basis for our efforts to address obstacles and crises, and makes it possible for us to come to terms with a range of predicaments and dilemmas that confront us in everyday life.

What are the features of this folk psychology? Perhaps first and foremost, it is distinguished by the notion of 'personal agency'. It casts people as active mediators, negotiators, and as representatives of their own lives, doing so separately and in unison with others. It is a psychology that is about people living their lives out according to certain intentions and purposes, in the pursuit of what matters to them. It is a psychology that is about people going about the business of satisfying certain wants and achieving sought after goals. It is a psychology that foregrounds matters of values and beliefs, and one that associates these values and beliefs with commitments to ways of life that characterise people. This emphasis on personal agency, on the significance that is assigned to notions of purpose, and on the weight that is given to notions of beliefs, values, and commitments, is a reflection of this folk psychology's theory of mind. In its appreciation of what it is that informs people's expressions of life, this tradition of folk psychology invokes 'mind'.[1]

In regard to traditions of understanding human life, folk psychology is one of many psychologies that are now available to people for these purposes. The last century or two has seen burgeoning developments in these traditions of human understanding, and many of these developments have had the effect of displacing, in some arenas, the tradition of folk psychology that I have been drawing out here. Others have changed the shape of some strains of folk psychology – folk psychology has not remained invariant, and has taken in many of the modern psychological notions that have been manufactured in this era of extraordinary expansion in the psychologies. However, in the face of these developments, the emphasis on the significance of personal agency and on intentional states is still strongly featured in the great majority of folk psychological accounts of human action.

The new psychologies

Although folk psychology has continued to enjoy a degree of popular success, it hasn't fared all that well in the arena of the professional psychologies. It is lowly ranked and marginalised by these psychologies. It is considered to be naïve in its conceptions of life and identity, mired in the biases of local culture, and non-scientific in the priority that it gives to the notions of human agency and intentional states. In the domain of the professional psychologies, folk psychology is considered not up to the sophistication and rigour required of a modern psychology for the development of adequate or, for that matter, even reasonable, understandings of human expression.

There have been many developments that have significantly impinged on the status of folk psychology in this way. The nineteenth century saw the bringing together, into a system of professional psychology, a number of 'modern' and interlinked developments of the preceding century or two. These included:

1. The development of humanist notions of the presence of a human 'nature' that is considered to be the foundation of personal existence, and that is understood to provide the source of human expression.

2. The evolution of the conception of a 'self' as an essence that is understood to occupy the centre of personal identity. Although this idea of a self is a relatively novel idea in the history of the world's cultures, it has been a hugely successful idea, and is today quite taken for granted in the west.

3. The progressive development, from the seventeenth century on, of a new system of social control in which the normalising judgement of people's lives has steadily displaced moral judgement.[2]

This new professional psychology was dismissive of the capacity of folk psychology to provide an adequately reasoned and rational explanation of human action. It de-emphasised the relevance of personal agency and intentional states. In the stead of these intentional state notions it substituted a notion of 'internal states' that were considered to be universal to the human condition.[3] Human expression was now interpreted as a surface manifestation of these internal states – a manifestation of unconscious motives, instincts, drives, traits, dispositions and so on. Various intrapsychic mechanisms (who hasn't heard of defence mechanisms) were constructed to provide an account of how these internal states were transformed into human expression. The development of these intrapsychic mechanisms provided the foundation of a new category of mind, the 'unconscious mind', and this quickly displaced the 'mind' of folk psychology.

Not all psychologies that construct intrapsychic mechanisms are founded on these internal state notions. For example, some fascinating developments in the exploration of mind were initiated during this era by psychologists of the ilk of William James (1890, 1892, 1902).[4] Although these developments featured various premises about what might be called intrapsychic processes, they did not construct internal state notions. This Jamesian tradition of understanding human life has been significantly renewed over the last decade or two. For example, see Russell Meares *Intimacy and Alienation* (2000).

In contrast to the 'intentional state' notions of folk psychology, and the psychologies influenced by James, notions of the internal state psychologies were increasingly taken up and applied to the identification of and treatment of a whole range of human maladies, the real causes of which were now considered inaccessible to ordinary human consciousness. These causes could only be discovered and known through archaeological processes guided by those equipped with the knowledge and skills in establishing the conditions under which true insight might be revealed. In many circles, these claims to the identification of an underlying and universal structure to human expression were heralded as a breakthrough in the scientific understanding of life and identity. Apart from anything else, these understandings of the new psychologies were considered to be beyond the culturally tainted understandings that are a characteristic of folk psychology. It was widely accepted that these developments would lay the foundations of a truly cross-cultural psychology.

Despite the early success of these internal state psychologies, they were soon faced with a significant challenge. During the period of World War One a new psychology emerged, one that consolidated itself in the 1920s and that became the dominant paradigm in professional psychology over the next two or three decades. This new psychology was a radical behaviourism that was inspired by the era of positivist science and by the extraordinary success of machine mechanics during the period encompassing the world wars. Radical behaviourism was dismissive of the traditions of psychology that preceded it, considering them irrational. This new psychology made concerted efforts to erase any notions of mind – folk conceptions of mind and the unconscious mind of internal state psychologies – in understandings of human action. In the domain of the professional disciplines it was largely successful in this objective (if not in popular imagination), for a time establishing virtual hegemony. The laboratory had become the context for human inquiry and for advancement in the psychology of what was now human 'behaviour', not human action.

In acknowledging the general success of radical behaviourism in its ambitions for professional psychology, I am not suggesting that it went unchallenged. There were many other developments in the psychologies that were questioning of the claims of radical behaviourism, but these were assigned little legitimacy and few avenues of expression.

Then came the so called 'cognitive revolution' of the 1950s, which initially endeavoured to erect meaning as a central tenant in psychology. It was in the context of this development that 'meaning' was accorded a priority in the understanding of human action. According to this, it was people's constructions of meaning that shaped their actions. An appreciation of how people went about making meaning out of their experiences of the world was considered the proper focus of a human psychology. Although this cognitive revolution successfully challenged the hegemony of the positivist behavioural traditions, as well as the personality theories of the internal state psychologies, unfortunately many of its early initiatives to install meaning as a central concept in psychology were subsequently derailed.[5]

Very soon, in what was no longer the era of machine mechanics in technology but the information era, this cognitive focus turned away from the production of meaning and onto 'information'. This shaped inquiry not into processes that people engage with in the construction of meaning but into the processing of information, not into the shape that these social constructions give to human expression but into the computation of information, and not into studies of the significance of constructions of meaning in regard to identity formation but into studies regarding precision in control inputs. As an outcome of these developments, notions of human agency and of intentional states were again rendered irrelevant to an adequate understanding of life and identity.

This brief account that I have given of the history of the development of traditions for understanding human action over the past century is partial. In the professional disciplines there have been many other developments, some of them relatively peripheral, and others that have, for a time, rivalled some of the more mainstream ideas. For example, most people who work in the family therapy field would be aware of the very significant influence of the 'new functionalism' of the 1950s, the legacy of which is so visible in many of the assumptions of 'systems theory' and in the practices of family therapy of recent decades. And I am sure that most people who work in this field would be aware of the spectacular success of cognitive behaviour therapy over the last decade or two. Since it is not possible for me in the space of this paper to draw an overview of developments such as these, I have had to be content to provide an account of a few of the specific, major, and historical mainstream developments that have played a significant role in displacing the relevance attributed to the mind of folk psychology in explanations of human action and expression.

Revival of the internal state psychologies

I came to my social work training in the wake of these developments. At this time, nothing much was settled. As a student studying psychology in 1967, I remember well being introduced to the claims of behaviourism and of information theory, to the debate surrounding these different representations of human action, and to some of the controversy associated with this debate. I was introduced to several versions of the internal state psychologies, including those that located these internal states in the 'family', not just the individual, and that provided the foundation for the manufacture of a new range of family pathologies and relationship dysfunctions. I was also introduced to the new functionalism in systems theory which also had the family as its primary focus. The only thing that did seem settled in the context of all of these claims and counter claims was this: In any consideration of human action and identity, notions of human agency and intentional states were irrelevant and inconsequential.

In the context of this climate, I am sure that readers could imagine, or perhaps even recall, the sort of reception provoked by the raising of unpopular lines of inquiry through questions like: 'And what about student participation in the anti-Vietnam war movement? Could this really be adequately explained away in the terms of unresolved family of origin issues? What if this was understood to be action that was principled, and therefore value and belief driven?'

In any case, whatever debate was taking place in the professional disciplines at this time, this was soon to be overshadowed by the phenomenal rise of the internal-state 'popular psychologies' in the late 1960s and early 1970s. These popular psychologies were not so much a resurgence of folk psychology, but an amalgam of:

- specific developments of the professional psychologies,
- aspects of the personal liberation philosophies that were the vogue of the 1960s,
- elements of the new consumer culture of the 1970s,
- bits of the structuralist developmental psychologies of Piaget and Erickson,
- pieces of Eastern spiritual and mystical traditions,
- facets of the new functionalism, and more.

What unified most of these popular psychologies was the status given to the self – the notion of 'essential self' was assigned an unquestioned status, even in the face of some extraordinary contradictions that this notion at times aroused in the realm of ideas and practice. It was a taken-for-granted fact that this was a self to be found at the centre of identity and that it existed independently of efforts to describe it.

This was the era of the great self revival. These popular psychologies were almost entirely 'self psychologies'. There was a self to be discovered at the core of personhood, one that was composed of certain essences that are of human nature. Life was considered to be either a direct expression of these essences, or, more often, a manifestation of the repression of, or distortion of, these essences. Strongly associated with this emphasis on the self was the catharsis injunction. At this time this injunction was the foremost of all psychological injunctions. Cathartic happenings were everywhere to behold, virtually pandemic. In fact, in some circles in the early 1970s, so all encompassing were the outbreaks of catharsis that it became virtually impossible to find social spaces untouched by this phenomenon in some way. These self psychologies were linked to this catharsis injunction through a powerful ethical obligation to discover the 'truth' of who one was and to seek to live a life that was an accurate and authentic expression of this truth.

Meaning, narrative and the reinstatement of folk psychology

In here describing the emergence of popular psychology, I am not suggesting that this idea about self as an essence was new – in fact it is a centuries old idea that significantly informed the internal state psychologies of the nineteenth century. And the quest for 'the truth of who we are' wasn't new either – it had been a major preoccupation of philosophical inquiry for several centuries. These developments of the 1960s and 1970s in popular psychology represented a resurgence and reinvigoration of some long-standing traditions of thought and practice. In recent times, these traditions have been enormously successful in capturing the popular imagination, and have undoubtedly influenced contemporary folk psychological understandings of life in many ways. However, many of these influences do not sit at all comfortably with those strains of folk psychology that emphasise human agency and intentional states, strains that remain ever present. These strains have remained highly visible in many domains of cultural life, including in the drama of much contemporary theatre and literature, especially the novel. As well, there have been a number of initiatives in recent decades to reinstate this tradition of folk psychology as a tradition relevant to inquiry in the human sciences and social sciences.

In fact, at the very time of the resurgence of internal state notions in the popular psychologies, some of the social sciences were going through what has been referred to as an 'interpretive turn' (Geertz 1973, 1983). It was in the context of this interpretive turn that meaning was placed firmly at the centre of social inquiry. This development was perhaps most visible in the emergence of the 'new' cultural anthropology. This was a form of inquiry based on the idea that people respond to each other in terms of their understandings of each others' actions, in terms of their own theories about what they and others are up to – that people respond to each other in terms of their own psychology. This premise placed the focus of inquiry firmly on meaning – on the constructions and categories of meaning that characterised communities of people. It brought the focus of inquiry to the significance of the meanings that people attributed to experiences of life. It sponsored studies into the life shaping effects of these meanings, and their role in the construction of people's identities.

With meaning at the centre, this new cultural anthropology took the focus of inquiry to the social construction of people's realities. These were realities that were not radically derived through one's independent construction of the events of one's life. These realities were not the outcome of some privileged access to the world as it is. They were not arrived at through some objective grasp of the nature of things. Rather, people's realities were understood to be historical and social products, negotiated in and between communities of people and distributed throughout these communities. This was the case for identity as much as for any other construction; identity was understood to be a phenomenon that was dispersed in communities of people, its traces to be found everywhere, including in:

- socially negotiated self narratives,
- the impressions and the imagination of others,
- the performance of drama,

- dance, in play, in song and in poetics,
- ritual, ceremony and symbol,
- attire and in habits of life, and
- personal and public documentation, dispersed through the inscriptions entered into community stories, into personal diaries, into correspondences in the form of letters and cards, into public files in the form of profiles, assessments and reports, and in the longstanding tradition of autobiography.

With meaning-making now at the heart of social inquiry, the very processes by which people rendered their experiences of their lives sensible to themselves and to each other began to receive significant attention. This focus was the outcome of understandings that meaning does not pre-exist the interpretation of experience, and that all meanings are linguistic and social achievements. This was also the outcome of the understanding that people give meaning to their experiences of life by taking these into frames that render them sensible or intelligible. The question that was raised in this inquiry was: 'What sort of frames of intelligibility are employed by people and by communities of people in their interpretive acts?'

The outcome of this exploration was a deepening appreciation of the extent to which people routinely construct meaning by trafficking in stories about their own and each others' lives, an appreciation that in turn lead to an understanding of the profoundly significant part that narrative structures play in providing a principle frame of intelligibility for everyday-life experience. People make sense of the world by taking their experiences of life into narrative frames, by locating these experiences in the familiar stories of their lives. In taking these experiences of life into narrative frames they become situated in sequences of events that are unfolding through time according to particular themes.

This development also reinstated the mind of folk psychology in understandings of people's acts of living. There is a homologous relationship between folk psychology notions of mind and the traditional structure of narrative. In the tradition of story-making and story-telling, agents are implicated in actions that are shaped by their intentional states and these actions have the objective of achieving certain goals. In the terms of this tradition of story telling, it is understood that the means employed in these strivings are influenced by and are revealing of what people believe, value, hope for and dream of. Taken together, these beliefs, values, hopes, and dreams come to represent what people's lives are about in general terms, and, in more specific terms, what they are committed to in terms how they wish to live their lives. The practices of life embraced by people in the pursuit of these sought after ends are seen to reflect their preferred ways of being in the world. In considerations of acts of life, the mind was back. And it was the mind of folk psychology, not a version of mind that invoked notions of internal states, of rational conception, of objective perception, of formal logic, or of the computation of information.

Before long this interpretive turn was gathering momentum in the social sciences, radically altering the shape of practices of inquiry into a whole range of social phenomena (for example, see Clifford 1988; Geertz 1973 1983; M. Rosaldo 1984; R. Rosaldo 1993; Turner & Bruner 1986). It also began to touch the human sciences (for example see Gergen & Gergen 1984; Spence 1982), and by the 1980s it had set off, in the social psychologies, numerous explorations into identity formation and human action. However, these developments in some of the human sciences did not much touch mainstream psychological and counselling practices over this time.

I believe that many of my own explorations of narrative therapy can be located within the context of this interpretive turn, and within this tradition of folk psychology. Many of the practices of this therapy routinely evoke notions of the personal agency and contribute to the rich description of a range of intentional states. These practices have the potential to bring forth the mindedness of folk psychology even in circumstances in which people's actions are routinely perceived to be discontinuous with what is known about them, and, on account of this, constructed as mindless or pathological or crazy. Practices that reinstate 'mindedness' also can have the effect of restoring people's cherished understandings and preferred identity claims, and can contribute to a range of options for people to respond to untoward events in ways that are in keeping with these preferred claims. I believe that the story of Jill and her family is illustrative of some of these practices.

Jill's family

I am meeting with Anne and David, and their son and daughter, Sam and Belinda for the first time. They have come to talk about a tragic event in their family – the death of their eldest daughter, Jill, through a fatal overdose that was not an accident, some three years ago. Things had gone okay in Jill's life for much of her childhood, but had then unravelled somewhat in her later years. Being from a relatively remote country region, she had gone away to school at twelve years of age, and things didn't work out all that well for her there. She struggled with peer abuse and with feelings of acute loneliness, but did not confide much of this to her parents. According to them, she eventually fell in with the wrong crowd, and seemed to embrace values that were totally at variance with those that she had grown up with, and which they could not understand.

The fact that she had been such a 'strong and adventurous and funny little kid' before things went so totally off the track had given Anne and David the sense that they had never really known Jill in her later years. Or was it that they hadn't really known her in her earlier years? It was all so confusing for them. Whichever the case, Anne and David felt badly about this. And Jill's distancing from them in the period leading up to her suicide had been very painful, particularly for Anne, who had such a strong sense of having failed Jill in her time of greatest need. Sam had also taken it very hard, as he felt that, over this time, there had been some opportunities to talk with Jill that he hadn't taken up.

Had it all been for nothing? It had become all just too sad and painful to think about, let alone to talk to each other about, and, as an outcome of this, the memory of Jill's existence was a rapidly diminishing sense for the members of this family. And no one in this family wanted to be on these terms with their memories of Jill.

Anne: So, I guess that this brings you up to the present, and why we decided to make this appointment. So where do we go? [throws arms into the air in an expression of despair]

M: Is it okay for me to ask some questions about the circumstances surrounding Jill's suicide?

Anne: Yeah. That's okay. We expected that you would want some of the details, didn't we [turning to David].

David: Yeah. We have been preparing ourselves for this.

M: [glancing at Sam and Belinda]

Sam: Yeah. It's okay. [turning to Belinda] Isn't it sis.

Belinda: [nods]

M: I have the sense from what you have been telling me that Jill was strongly resolved to do this. To take her own life. I was thinking about all the thought that she must have put into it, and about the preparations that were …

Anne: That's true. Yes.

David: [nods]

M: Were these sort of actions in character for Jill?

Anne: Well, I don't know. I don't think that she really prepared for much at all really. I'm just thinking about how everything went off the rails, you know.

M: What about occasions upon which she was strongly resolved to do something big or difficult or daunting, that she followed through on? Can you think of any?

Anne: Well … I … [looks to David] Can you?

David: This has me thinking of other times. Yeah. When she was younger, she was really plucky. She really was a plucky little kid. Wasn't she?

Anne: That's true.

David: Do you remember that time we were at the beach. She must have been four years old, and it was time to go, and she was carrying all of those toys and her hat and her clothes and trying to eat a sandwich at the same time as she was trying to get up those sand hills. And you knew she wouldn't let anyone help. And along came a woman who scowled at us. One of those telling off looks. She tried to pick things up for Jill. You remember.

Anne: Yeah. Yeah. [smiling] Jill shouted: 'It's my life!' And she was only four years old! Can you believe that? She was only four years old! And what did she do? She just chucked everything back down the hill again, the sandwich and all, and then went tumbling after them, trying to grab them all up again as she went, much to this woman's horror. [Anne is now laughing, along with David]

David: There she was standing at the bottom, all covered in sandwich and sand, and grinning from ear to ear.

Belinda: [laughing] Yeah, I've heard that story before.

Sam: I can think of lots of others just like that one. [also laughing]

M: So when thinking about the strength of her resolve, it doesn't totally surprise you? The way that she took her life, I mean.

Anne: Well, actually no. I guess not. Not really. But I reckon she had lost this for a while.

David: Yeah, for sure.

M: So, it sort of fits with the plucky person she was. And anything else?

Anne: Well I don't know what this has got to do with it. But she always kept trying at things when others would give up. When she was younger that is.

Belinda: Yeah. But also when she was older. I remember how hard it was for her with all of the teasing she went through. It would have been better if she'd let us do something about it, but she wouldn't have it. But she sure didn't give up trying to tackle it. She went against it, didn't she? She didn't just accept this. She had these ideas about what was right and fair, about what was okay and what wasn't.

Sam: Yeah, that's sure true in one way, but …

David: But then she got into some bad things and did some things that really were really scary and not okay, that caused other people a lot of pain and heartache. So, I don't know … It just doesn't make sense, does it?

M: I wonder how this fits in. If it does fit in, that is.

David: What do you mean?

M: Belinda said something about where Jill stood on what was right and what wasn't, on what was okay and what wasn't okay. If Jill had witnessed herself doing things that went against these values, how would this be for her?

David: Actually, I reckon this would have been difficult for her. She wouldn't have been at all happy with herself.

M: Do you have any thoughts about whether or not this could relate to the decisions that Jill was making about her life prior to her death?

Anne: I didn't think about this, but maybe there is something in it. I reckon that she went against so many of her principles, and in lots of ways she did this. So, maybe there is some connection, that this was in a funny way about her principles. It could have been, it really could have.

M: I want to check to see if I am getting your meaning. Are you saying that there may have been something about taking her life that was principled? Not in the way that anyone would have wished, but …

David: Yeah. I guess … like Anne said, in funny sort of way. I guess that is what we are saying [sighs].

M: [turning to Anne, who had echoed David's sigh] Anne, is that where are you with this?

Anne: Yeah. This is something I can see. But I am really surprised to hear myself admitting this. Shocked even.

M: You both sighed. Could I ask what these sighs are about?

Anne: It's a strange sense of relief really. I mean there would have been a lot of other ways for her to do something. But this is something to hold onto, and … well, I am desperate for that, totally desperate for that.

M: David?

David: For me too. Some relief I guess.

M: Going back to the circumstances of her death, I understand that she distanced from you in the period leading up to this. And that this was very hard for all of you.

Anne: [starts crying]

M: Would you say something about those tears? Would you help me understand what they are about?

Anne: [pause] I was thinking about my connection with Jill. I thought that we had always been so close. But I must have been wrong. [pause] I can't help but feel that I not only failed to understand, but that I failed her.

M: Tell me. How did you reach this conclusion?

Anne: Because she didn't come to me in what must have been her time of greatest need. I'm sure that I failed her [sobbing] [pause]. Even though the special relationship that we once had was gone, well … anyway, clearly she didn't think that she could rely on me or that I had anything to offer.

M: Did anyone else here also think that there was a special connection between Anne and Jill?

Belinda: Yeah. Sure. Sure there was. She was always sending mum cards and things, [turning to Sam] wasn't she?

Sam: Yeah. If she was going to tell anyone anything, it was mum she would tell.

M: So what's your sense of how she regarded her connection with your mum?

David: She just treasured it, I know it. That's so clear to me as well. To all of us [Belinda and Sam nod in agreement].

M: Okay. So, in the light of this, what sense do you make out of this distancing from Anne in the period leading up to her death? Would this distance have made it more or less possible for Jill to take her life?

David: I don't know if this is right but I think that I've got an answer for that. I don't reckon that there is anyway that Jill could have followed through on this decision to end her life if she had been close to Anne at the time, and I reckon that Jill knew this. I'm not saying things were perfect. I know that there were some hard times and some differences, you know the usual sort of thing … But she just treasured her relationship with her mother.

M: So, there could have been a purpose to this distancing from Anne, and from the rest of you? That …

David: Yeah. Now that I think about it, I'm sure of it.

Sam: I can see it too.

Anne: [now sobbing]

David: [holding her in his arms, also crying]

M: In some way – and I know this might sound like a strange way of putting it – from what you are saying it is my understanding that this distancing may have been a testimony to Jill's connection with Anne? Can I check this understanding with you?

Sam: [also crying] Yeah, I can see this too

Belinda: [also crying] Me too.

M: [also tearful] You have given me a strong sense of what your tears are about. But I would like to ask a couple of questions about what's happening for you? Is that okay?

Anne: It is okay.

M: I know that you have had lots of tears. These tears that you are having now, are these the same tears? Or are they different tears?

Anne: For me they are different.

M: Okay, so they are different tears for you. Are they taking you to the same place though, or to a different place. To where you have been before, or are they journeying you to somewhere else?

Anne: It is to a different place.

M: Would you be prepared to tell me about this, or would you prefer not to?

Anne: It is to a place where … let's see … I still feel very sad. But it is different somehow. How is it different? [pause] Well … these tears are not taking me down that well and into the void, into the nothingness that I feel that I have been drowning in. It is easier … these tears that is, and it is with some new thoughts, taking me into a … yes ... a lighter place. [pause] I am sure that I will never lose this sadness, but if I can hold on to what I am feeling now,

I know that I am not going to be so overwhelmed. And yes [pause]. Of course, there are lots of good memories.

M: I was just …

Anne: There is something else … yeah … I've got something back that I thought I had lost. And I didn't expect this, I really didn't.

M: What's your guess about how Jill would be responding to this, responding to this development?

Anne: Well …

Belinda: She would want this for mum. [turning to Anne] Mum, she would want this for you so much, I just know she would [turning to Sam] Wouldn't she Sam?

Sam: Yeah, and for us too.

M: Do you mean that she wouldn't want the fact of her death to take away from …

Belinda: Her connection with all of us.

Sam: Yeah.

M: Would it be okay if I asked some questions that could have the effect of evoking Jill's presence here? Because I would like to get a sense of the words that she might use to say all of this, and a sense of the way that she would say it. I had some other ideas for our conversation as well. I am curious to know more about how your lives are different for having had Jill as daughter and as a sister. Because it is my guess that this has changed you all in some way, that there are some ways that you think and that you are in this world that are a testimony to her life. Would these directions fit for you, or do you have some other ideas about where it might be best for us to go now?

The family members wanted to follow up both of these lines of inquiry, and this provided a basis for some extraordinary conversations over the course of three or four meetings. Following this Anne and David called a gathering of extended family and friends for the purposes of honouring Jill's life and the legacy of her life. In the context of this ceremony, Anne, David, Sam and Belinda talked openly of Jill's suicide, rendering this and the events surrounding it sensible to all present in terms of what they understood she had lived for, in terms of what they understood she had stood for in her life, and in terms of the significance of her relationships with the members of her family. In this ceremony, the conclusions it appeared Jill had reached that called for her suicide were acknowledged. Even though her death would always be powerfully lamented, there was now some acknowledgement of the fact that Jill's suicide did fit with many of the things that they knew of her, and that it wasn't mindless or crazy. Anne, David, Sam and Belinda successfully renegotiated the terms of their memories of Jill. The facts of her existence, and the significance of this to their lives, were experiences that could now be readily called upon by them all.

I believe that this account of my conversations with Jill's family illustrates the sort of options that become available to people when space is created for the generation of the 'mindedness' of folk psychology. It was in the context of these conversations, through explorations that were deriving of notions of personal agency and intentional states, that Jill's actions were rendered mindful. These were explorations that were consistent with a reinstatement of the 'mind' of the folk psychology traditions that I have been describing in this paper.

Part Two

Personal agency and intentional states

In several places in this paper I have made reference to the significance that is attributed to notions of personal agency and intentional states in the context of narrative explorations of human action and identity formation. At this juncture I will make a number of clarifications about what is being proposed in this. I believe that this is appropriate because this emphasis on the significance of these notions of personal agency and intentional states is often construed as a proposal for traditions of understanding that do not fit at all well with the folk psychology tradition that I have been describing. In attending to these clarifications I will draw attention to the part that therapeutic practices shaped by this folk psychology tradition can play in the production of 'multi-intentioned' lives, of 'joined' lives, of 'multiple authenticities', and of 'inhabited' lives.

The production of multi-intentioned lives

At times the emphasis given to notions of personal agency and intentional states in narrative practices is read as a proposal for:

1. strictly rational understandings of life,
2. the privileging of contemporary ideas about individual and autonomous thought and action,
3. a renewal of the internal state psychologies in which these intentional states are re-cast as a phenomena that are intrinsic to people's lives, or for
4. the revival of highly deterministic cause/effect accounts of human action.

However, this is not what is being proposed. Rather, this 'take' on personal agency and intentional states is to propose that, in response to a person's expressions of life, there is a range of opportunities for people to engage with each other in the negotiation and renegotiation of the sort of identity conclusions that are informed by a tradition of folk psychology. It is in this tradition that notions of personal agency and intentional states are attributed to and implicated in people's acts of living. These notions of personal agency and intentional states are present in those conclusions about people's actions that are shaped by categories of identity that feature purposes, values, beliefs, hopes, dreams, visions and commitments to ways of living. These categories of identity can be likened to 'filing cabinets' of the mind, into which people routinely file and cross reference a range of identity conclusions about their own and each other's lives.

These identity conclusions are not independently and autonomously manufactured, but are socially negotiated and renegotiated in communities of people. And they are not singular. These identity conclusions exist within the context of a multiplicity – as an outcome of the ongoing social negotiation of these identity conclusions, people's lives become multi-intentioned. This emphasis on the significance of the social negotiation of people's identity conclusions is not reproducing of internal state notions. These identity conclusions are not taken to be a reflection of phenomena that are intrinsic to people's lives that are manifested in their actions. Rather, what is being proposed is that it is these conclusions themselves that have consequences for people's lives and relationships. People's acts of living, including their responses to each other, are shaped by the identity conclusions that are filed into the identity categories of the mind, which are circumscribed by contemporary culture's favoured notions of identity. These identity conclusions significantly constitute people's existence.

For the purposes of further clarification, I will here contrast the opportunities that I believe folk psychology offers for the renegotiation of identity conclusions with those associated with the internal state psychologies. The categories of identity associated with notions of personal agency and intentional states are distinct in relation to those of the internal state psychologies categories of 'motives', 'drives', 'needs', 'attributes', 'traits', and so on. In the context of the internal state psychologies, human expression is understood to be a surface manifestation of some essence or force or element that resides at the centre of identity, or to be a manifestation of a distortion or disturbance or imbalance in these forces. In the context of people's difficulties in life, these expressions are invariably considered to be expressions of pathology, deficit or dysfunction. It is upon the basis of such conclusions that many of the knowledges of the professional disciplines, and the systems of analyses that are constructed through these knowledges, are called forth. It is proposed that through recourse to these systems of analyses the pathologies, disorders and dysfunctions of people's lives can be identified and definitively known, and that these then can be subject to 'treatments of choice'.

In contrast, I believe that the intentional states of folk psychology are radically open to the sort of renegotiations that have the potential to throw people's expressions of life into a multiplicity of different lights. When it comes to people's difficulties in life, in the context of these intentional state understandings, human action is not indicative of disturbances of the internal states. Rather, these difficulties raise options for people to traffick in conceptions of personal agency and intentional states notions, and in this there are options for the attribution of alternative purposes not previously appreciated, for the restoration of cherished understandings and preferred identity claims (as in the story of my work with Jill's family), and for the elaboration of moral commitments that diverge from those that have been previously acknowledged. In the context of these understandings nothing is settled – considerations of life are taken into the subjunctive, a great deal is open to renegotiation, diversity is emphasised, and people's lives become multi-purposed and multi-layered.

The production of joined lives

Externalising conversations are often, but not always, featured in the practices of narrative therapy. In response to the problems of their lives, it is not uncommon for people to form highly negative conclusions about their own and each other's identity, and about the identity of their relationships. It is in these circumstances that externalising conversations open options for people to redefine or revise their relationships with the problems of their lives, and to so break their lives from these highly negative identity conclusions. In this redefinition of one's relationship with problems, the negative identity conclusions that invariably invoke some internal state of some sort – usually associated with some account of deficit, pathology, or dysfunction – no longer speak to people of the totality of who they are. It is in the context of these conversations that people derive a sense that their identity is not at one with the problems of their lives. Amongst other things, this opens space for yet other conversations that contribute to the generation of alternative stories of people's lives, and to the renegotiation of identity conclusions. People invariably respond to these conversations by engaging in the performance of some of the preferred claims about their lives that are associated with these alternative identity conclusions.

I have always regarded these alternative identity conclusions that are derived in these conversations to be socially negotiated in communities of people, and to be products of history and culture. I raise this point here because, despite the care that I have taken in my writing and teaching to consistently emphasise the social basis of these alternative identity conclusions, it is sometimes assumed that these externalising conversations are associated with the proposal of an autonomous self that is being freed from the oppression of the problem. I believe that the vigour of this assumption is a reflection of the pervasiveness of western culture's taken-for-granted understandings that construct a self at the centre of personhood.

I believe that the proposal of an autonomous self has been strongly supported in the development of the internal state psychologies. If it is so that the proposal of the autonomous self is associated with modern developments in the cellularisation of life (and this is argued quite convincingly by many historians of thought), the internal state categories of identity contribute to developments in the sub-cellularisation of life. According to Foucault (1973, 1979), the proposal of the autonomous self seems closely associated with the development of modern systems of social control in which people are separated from each other by being allocated precise locations in a range of continuums of health and tables of performance – locations that specify one's distance from the socially constructed and desirable norms regarding the healthy and fully functioning individual. It would appear that the proposal of internal state categories of identity take the cellularisation a step further – the autonomous individual is separated into relatively autonomous internal states that life becomes an expression of. As an outcome of this development, people are alone in their 'motives', isolated in their 'deficits', and vulnerable in their 'psychological needs'.

In contrast, I believe externalising conversations that contribute to options for people to separate from the sort of negative identity conclusions that invoke accounts of deficit, pathology and dysfunction, and re-authoring conversations that provide opportunities for people to generate new identity conclusions that feature folk psychological notions of personal agency and intentional states, have the potential to overturn this cellularisation of life. Rather than contributing to the sort of internal state conclusions that are potentially isolating of people from each other, these conversations contribute to the development of identity conclusions that provide people with a sense of their lives being joined with the lives of others around shared themes that are characterised by a range of purposes, values, beliefs, hopes, dreams, visions, commitments, and so on (in this respect, consider how transporting the therapeutic conversation was for Paul – from being isolated in his deficits to becoming joined with his mother's life around shared purposes and skills).

In summary, therapeutic conversations that provide options for people to traffick in intentional state notions raise new possibilities for the joining of identities, provide an antidote to the normalising judgement that is so intimately associated with the development of the autonomous self, and contribute to the de-cellularisation of life.

The production of multiple authenticities

In discussing the processes of therapy, I have from time to time made reference to dominant and alternative stories, and frequently contrasted these (for example, see White 1989, 1992). There have been many occasions in which others have taken this distinction into humanist renderings. These are renderings that substitute 'dominant story' with 'oppressive' or 'false story', and that substitute 'alternative story' with 'true' or 'real' or 'authentic' story. In these renderings the alternative stories of people's lives are accorded a naturalistic status in much the same vein that this status is attributed to the identity categories of the internal state psychologies. By this account it is understood that the conversations of narrative therapy are libratory conversations – it is considered that these conversations make it possible for people to overthrow the oppressive stories of their lives, and provide a context for the discovery and unveiling of their true or authentic stories. At times these renderings of the dominant- story/alternative-story distinction endure, despite the fact that this is contrary to what I have proposed, and the fact that many of the ideas associated with narrative therapy raise very specific questions about such renderings.

Rather than contrast stories as oppressive and authentic or as false and true, I have been interested in the constitutive or shaping effects of all stories. Stories about life and identity are not equal to each other in their constitutive effects. It is clearly apparent that some stories sponsor a broader range of options for action in life than do others. For example, I am sure that everyone would appreciate the fact that the deficit-centred stories of people's lives sponsor a particularly narrow range of options for action. In addition to my interest in the constitutive or shaping effects of all stories, I have been interested in conversational processes that are richly describing of those stories of people's lives that open more options for action in the world rather than fewer. It is in the context of these conversations that people not only experience their lives as multi-storied, but clearly become more narratively resourced. It is in the context of becoming more narratively resourced that people are able to attribute significance to a range of experiences of life that would otherwise be neglected.

In calling into question the rendering of the dominant story/alternative story distinction that establishes the juxtaposition of oppressive and real or authentic stories, and that casts therapeutic conversations as libratory, what becomes of the notion of authenticity? Rather than understanding authenticity to be a phenomenon that is discovered as an outcome of some private and individual achievement in which the 'truth' of a person's identity is revealed, or as an outcome of the identification of their 'true' story, within the context of the tradition of thought associated with narrative therapy, authenticity is regarded as a public and social achievement in which a person's preferred identity claims are acknowledged. It is understood that people are dependent upon social processes of acknowledgement for the 'authentication' of their preferred identity claims; that, as an outcome of this social acknowledgement, people experience being 'at one' with these preferred claims.

Preferred claims about people's identities are embedded in the alternative stories of their lives, and therapeutic conversations that are structured by the 'definitional ceremony' metaphor (Myerhoff 1982, 1986) present a range of options for the rich description of these stories.[6] These are conversations that engage people as outsider witnesses in the telling and retelling of the stories of each others' lives. It is in the context of these tellings and retellings that people experience themselves being at one with the preferred claims about their identities. Therapeutic practices that are shaped by this understanding contribute to the development of circumstances under which a range of preferred identity claims can be acknowledged, under which there are options for people to experience 'multiple authenticities'.

The outsider witnesses that contribute to retellings of the stories of people's lives that are powerfully authenticating of their preferred identity claims can be drawn from these people's families and wider kinship networks, from their friendship networks, from the professional disciplines, from the local community, from lists or registers of people who have previously sought therapeutic consultation and who have volunteered to contribute to the therapist's work with those who follow in their footsteps, and from elsewhere.[7] Jill's family called together friends and extended family members to a ceremony that was honouring of Jill's life and actions. This ceremony was structured around a series of tellings and retellings of the stories of Jill's life. These tellings and retellings were powerfully authenticating of the preferred identity claims about the lives and relationships of the members of this family, and of their sense of Jill's ongoing presence in their lives.

The production of inhabited lives

There appears to be intimate link between narrative structures and the fantastic capacity that people have for reflexive engagements with life. This reflexivity is a capacity to achieve distance in relation to the immediacy of life. It is witnessed in our ability to stand out of the flow of lived experience, sometimes only momentarily, and to review the events of our lives from other vantage points. It is largely in the reading of our lives as lived through the structure of narrative that we are afforded the purchase to stand back from our lives. This reading of our lives through narrative structures provides the opportunity for us to render meaningful that which previously wasn't, and to re-conceive of that which has already been rendered meaningful. This generation and regeneration of meaning allows for a sense of narrative authority, and for an experience of living that people describe as akin to stepping in and out of the flow of life.

This generation and regeneration of meaning also occurs across time. Our reflexive capacity provides us with new alternatives for what to make out of:

1. the past in response to any new meanings that are assigned to our experiences of the present,
2. the present in response to any new meanings that are assigned to our experiences of the past,
3. the future in response to any new meanings that are assigned to our experiences of the past and/or the present, and
4. the past and/or the present in response to any new meanings assigned to proposed or hypothetical futures.

An example: Those therapeutic conversations which are tracing of the history of a unique outcome or exception through the trajectory of a person's life often introduce options for a creative re-engagement with one's past. This is a re-engagement that provides possibilities for the identification of purposes that were not previously fully grasped, of commitments not previously felt, and of moral considerations that were previously unconsidered. In turn, it is through these recountings that people arrive at new understandings of current predicaments and dilemmas, of why events took the turn that they did, and of what these might mean for the future of their lives. All this occurs in the backwards and forwards movement of therapeutic conversations.

When in the past I have described various options that therapeutic conversations can provide for these reflexive re-engagements with life, at times it has been assumed by others that narrative practices deal with abstractions of life, rather than life itself – that this contributes to a certain therapist detachment in therapeutic practice, and requires the people who consult therapists to participate in therapeutic conversations in a detached fashion that takes them away from more direct expressions of their experiences of life. However, detachment is not synonymous with the sort of distance that provides opportunities for the reflexive engagements with life that I have described in the above paragraphs. The distance that is achieved in the reading of life through narrative structures is one that provides people with wonderful opportunities for a more significant and dramatic engagement with their own lives. It is a distance that opens possibilities for people to explore new options in self regulation, and in the habitation of their own bodies. It is a distance that presents options for people to more fully inhabit their lives, as the following account of my conversations with Ricky illustrates.

Ricky

Ricky consulted me over a personal crisis following a recent relationship break-up. This break-up had occurred eleven months before our first consultation. At the time, Peter, Ricky's partner of seven years, suddenly announced his intention to depart from the relationship, declaring that he had never really loved Ricky. He then listed his complaints and dissatisfactions with Ricky, about which he had never previously spoken of, or even hinted about. Peter's parting comment was that Ricky and relationships don't go together. Ricky was shattered: 'Is there anywhere that one can go from here when so racked with self-doubt, with one's sense of ability to judge the intentions of others in tatters, and with one's trust in ruins? Is there anywhere that one can go from here with all of this baggage, quite apart from the loss that one is experiencing?' Ricky concluded that his ability to trust had been damaged beyond repair, and he began to stand back from his social network. A friend had responded to this by talking Ricky into seeing me.

Ricky: So, there you are. All of this was shattering. Apart from everything else, it has taken away my trust. It is a fear of trusting. I have this inability to trust, and … well, you know … I think it has damaged me. And I don't know if I could ever learn to trust again.

M: Would you say a little more about this. About this sense of a loss of trust, or an inability to trust?

Ricky: It is like, well ... like I just feel that I can't fully trust anymore, and what's life going to be like for me, because I am not getting over this. I feel like I am stuck with this deficit.

M: Is this something that has become evident to you in your connections with others? Has it been noticed by any of your friends?

Ricky: Yeah. That's how I got to here, seeing you. Only the other day I was talking to a friend who felt that I was being a bit guarded. And they said, this friend, that is, said: 'You have a problem with trust. You should see someone about this.'

M: And so here you are. I understand that Peter's announcement and his subsequent actions were quite unexpected at the time. Looking back, are you aware of anything that might have prepared you for what was to come.

Ricky: I suppose, but you know what they say about hindsight.

M: It is always easy to be wise …

Ricky: Yeah. It is always easy to be wise after the event, isn't it.

M: Tell me about some of that wisdom of hindsight.

Ricky: Well, of course, I should have seen it coming, shouldn't I. And I have been giving myself a hard time over this, haven't I.

M: Are you telling me that there are some things that you are conscious of now, or aware of now, that you were not before?

Ricky: You could say that. Yeah, I guess that would be right. At least I hope that is right. Well, a wish, maybe. Perhaps even that's a bit strong.

M: If faced with similar circumstances today, and being aware of what you are now aware of, perhaps even to the extent of being able to predict such a turn of events, do you think that you would be investing so much trust in a relationship? Would this be appropriate?

Ricky: No. No, it wouldn't. I would withhold it. But then, I didn't see I coming then, so how could I do this? Well, I really don't know, do I?

M: Let's just speculate. If you did see something like this coming, what would you be doing with this trust? What sort of attitude would you be having towards this trust?

Ricky: I am not sure what you mean.

M: Would withholding trust in such a circumstance suggest that you were putting a high value on your trust or a low value on it, respecting it more or less, preserving it or being reckless with it, or holding it back or … Or perhaps none of these, but something else maybe?

Ricky: Well, thinking about it like that, I would say the other ones. The first ones. I would say that I would be being respectful of my trust, that I would be valuing it more.

M: You said that you had become guarded in your present day-to-day connections with people, so I have the sense that you haven't just continued to live your life as you had previously lived it, and that you haven't cast your trust about freely in an attempt to recreate the life that you had. In the light of what we have just been talking about, what are your thoughts about what this says about your position on trust?

Ricky: Let's see. Well, I can only think that I am, well, let's see, maybe cherishing this trust now. Do you think that I am cherishing this trust more? [pause] Yeah, I guess that is it.

M: Okay. Does this mean that you now wouldn't make this trust so available to others in certain circumstances, or that …

Ricky: Yeah. Look, I didn't think that I would hear myself saying this, but I guess that is what I am saying.

M: Why didn't you think that you would hear yourself saying this?

Ricky: Because it is nothing that I would have put to words before. There really is a shift here, but I really hadn't stood back from it and given much thought to this until now. I mean until right this minute.

M: Do you have any thoughts about why you have been cherishing this trust more? And about what it might say about other developments in your life?

Ricky: I suppose it is about a ... [pause] Yeah, more of a determination to be respected. Yeah, that's probably it. And perhaps I'm not going to let it be taken for granted. My trust, that is. I've had enough of that, I have.

M: Anything else that this might reflect? Like …

Ricky: Well, like what?

M: What's your guess about what this says about your purposes, or about what you value?

Ricky: Maybe it is that I don't intend to give up on how I want to live my life.

M: On how you want to life your life? Tell me, of all the people who have known you, can you think of anyone who might have appreciated these things about you? Who might have appreciated this determination, or who might have acknowledged the choices that you made about how you wanted to live your life?

Ricky: Well …

Ricky identified two figures of his history who he believed had appreciated him in these terms – an ex-lover and an aunt. I encouraged him to provide accounts of what it was that these figures might have witnessed that could have contributed to this appreciation of him. The accounts given by Ricky established a basis for yet further explorations about what it was he had intended for his life. Following this meeting, Ricky contacted this ex-lover and his aunt, told them about our conversation, and shared with them his conclusions about how their acknowledgement of him had contributed to his life. For our third meeting, at Ricky's invitation, we were joined by these two people.

Apart from other things, these conversations provided a foundation for establishing a clear account of the circumstances under which Ricky would be prepared to offer trust in his connections with others, and the circumstances under which this trust would not be available. He subsequently met again with the friend that he had mentioned early in our first conversation. In this meeting, Ricky described the circumstances that he understood were favourable and unfavourable to his trusting of others, and informed this friend that in any act in which he extended this trust he was presenting a gift that was offered provisionally. This led to some significantly new and positive developments in this connection. Ricky no longer had a sense of having 'a problem with trust'.

This brief description of my conversations with Ricky provides an account of the way that narrative structures can provide a foundation for reflexive engagements with life. Upon being encouraged to speculate about his likely responses should he have been conscious of what he hadn't been conscious of in his relationship with Peter, Ricky concluded that he would have withheld trust. This conclusion provided the basis for a flurry of meaning-making activity in which Ricky's responses to the day-to-day events of his life were redefined, in which specific developments in his relationship to trust were named, and in which what this reflected about his intentions for his life were determined and richly described.

In these therapeutic conversations, the structure of narrative provided Ricky with purchase to stand back from life and to re-conceive of that which had already been rendered meaningful. This provided a frame for a regeneration of meaning in which constructions of integrity displaced constructions of deficit. It was from the distance achieved in this reflexive engagement that Ricky was able to discern the circumstances under which this trust would be available to others. And the subsequent performance of this discernment in his conversation with his friend is an example of the way that the distance achieved through reflexive engagements provide possibilities for people to more fully inhabit some of the domains of their own lives. Amongst other things, these are possibilities in the regulation of their own actions in response to the actions of others.

In the next and final section of this paper, I will turn to considerations of history and culture.

Part Three

History and culture

> *To argue that culture is socially and historically constructed, that narrative is a primary, in humans perhaps the primary mode of knowing, that we assemble the selves we live in out of materials lying about in the society around us and develop a theory of mind to comprehend the selves of others, that we do not act directly on the world but on beliefs we hold about the world, that from birth on we are all active, impassioned meaning makers in search of plausible stories, and that mind cannot in any sense be regarded as natural or naked, with culture thought of as an add-on – such a view amounts to rather more than a midcourse correction.* (Geertz 2000, p.196).

In various places in this paper I have addressed the notion that life is a social phenomenon. For example, I have reviewed how constructions of life and identity are socially negotiated in communities of people, and I have drawn attention to the central role that processes of social acknowledgement play in the authentication of people's identity claims. But life is also a social phenomenon in that it is the outcome of people's engagements with specific modes of thought and life that are cultural and historical. These modes of thought and life compose life.

Our understandings of life and identity are not arrived at in an historical and cultural vacuum. Whether these understandings pertain to our sense of personal identity, to our accounts of other people's actions, to what one might do to change the way things are, or whatever, they are all informed by specific ways of thinking that are based on a stock of cultural knowledges. Not only are these knowledges historical and cultural products, but so too are the skills that are evident in our ways of living, in our acts of life. I am using the word 'skills' in an unconventional sense – these are those skills that are represented in all of those little everyday acts of life that have to do with the making of a 'living', with getting through the day, with the forging of an identity, and with the fabricating of relationships. It is only through such a definition of skills that we can conceive of what might be referred to as practical 'insider know-how', that we can come to fully appreciate this know-how in the lives of the people who consult us, and that we can join with people in the co-researching of what might be described as 'local knowledge'.

These skills are shaped by cultural modes of living that include specific practices of relationship – for example, those practices that constitute relations of power – and specific practices of self-formation, at times referred to as 'technologies of the self' or 'disciplines of the self' (Foucault 1979). These practices of relationship and practices of self formation are linked to cultural knowledges of life and identity in relationships of mutual dependency.

Over many years of writing and teaching, following Foucault I have drawn attention to the relationship between these knowledges and cultural practices, and to their constitutive role in expressions of life (for example see White & Epston 1989). And I have also described and illustrated the relevance of these considerations to the practice of therapy. However, at times these considerations pertaining to the relationship between knowledge and practice or knowledge and power ('power' on account of the fact that many of these practices constitute relations of power) have, in my view, been misinterpreted. For example:

1) When I am describing the relations of mutual dependency of these knowledges and practices, it is at times assumed that what is being proposed is a new version of that familiar refrain: power is knowledge and knowledge is power.

2) When drawing attention to the constitutive role of cultural knowledges and cultural practices in the formation of life and identity, it is at times assumed that I am proposing a direct causal relationship between these knowledges and practices and people's expressions of living – that people's expressions of living are directly determined by these knowledges and practices.

3) When describing and illustrating the relevance of these considerations to a therapeutic practice that brings into focus to the stories of people's lives, it is at times assumed that I am conflating the idea of narrative with these cultural knowledges and practices, serving to obscure many things, including the power relations of local culture.

In order to further emphasise the significance of this understanding that life is a social phenomenon that is constituted through specific modes of life and thought that are historical and cultural, and to further clarify these considerations pertaining to knowledge and practice, I will address these three relatively common misinterpretations in turn.

Power / Knowledge

Contrary to interpretations that substitute knowledge with power and power with knowledge, attempts to describe the relations of mutual dependency between these culturally informed knowledges on the one hand, and these practices of relationship and techniques of the self on the other, do not lend themselves at all well to the familiar refrain 'knowledge is power and power is knowledge'. In explorations of these practices of relationship and techniques of self, our attention is drawn to relational practices, and to a 'know-how', that is manifest in skilful practice of life. Although these practices and skills are linked to and supported by certain cultural constructs, they are not in themselves constructs. When I meet with men who are referred to me for engaging in abusive actions, these actions are shaped by a technology of power, which is a practical know-how that is shaped by specific skills. These skills make possible the overpowering of whoever happens to be the subject of these actions (usually women and children), the isolation of this subject from others, the destruction of this subject's trust in their own perception of events, the assignment of culpability for the abuse to the subject, and so on. Although these actual relational practices are linked to and supported by knowledges that construct, amongst other things, male supremacy and entitlement, they are not one and the same.

Another example: When I am engaged in therapeutic conversations with people who are struggling with anorexia nervosa and bulimia (usually, but not always, women) I am introduced to concepts of identity and to constructions of the body that are informed by knowledges of life that are of contemporary culture. I am also introduced to a history of relational practices, which, amongst other things, include various operations of power that these people have been subject to. As well, I am introduced to a range of techniques of the self that include self evaluation, the precise documentation of inputs and outputs (of all manner of things from calories through to one's thoughts), the rigorous policing of one's life that makes possible the achievement of 'life as ritual', and so on. Again, although these relational practices and techniques of self formation are linked to and find their support in cultural knowledges that construct life and identity, they cannot be reduced to these knowledges. Rather these practices are linked to cultural knowledges through relations of mutual dependency. This consideration is highly relevant to therapeutic conversations, for it calls attention to the importance of not only addressing people's constructions of their own and each others' identities, but also to the importance of addressing the very practices of relationship and techniques of self that accompany these constructions.

Indeterminacy within determinacy

In regard to these observations about the constitutive role of cultural knowledges and practices in the formation of life, what about those conclusions that assume that what is being proposed is a direct causal relationship between these knowledges and practices on the one hand, and people's expressions of life on the other? Attention to the constitutive role of cultural knowledges and cultural practices in the formation of life and identity is not necessarily associated with an assumption that life and identity are strictly determined by cultural modes of life and thought – attention to these considerations is not necessarily associated with the proposal that there is a one-to-one relationship between these cultural knowledges and practices on the one hand, and life as it is lived on the other. In fact, I have always assumed that this is not the case – that in constructing their lives and identities, people do not passively reproduce these cultural knowledges and practices. I have never considered these knowledges of life and practices of living to be 'inputs' that are directly reproduced as 'outputs' in people's acts of life. Rather, considerations of the constitutive role of cultural knowledges and practices have provoked my interest in questions like:

- *How do people engage with these cultural modes of life and thought?*
- *How do these cultural forces that are composed of knowledges of life and practices of living find their way into people's minds and into their expressions of life?*

- *How is it that people pull the materials of culture together to form an identity, to make a life?*
- *If expressions of life are versions of these knowledges and practices, how are these versions achieved?*

It is questions like these that have lead me to further explorations of meaning making. For it is so clearly apparent that in engaging with these cultural modes of life and thought, in pulling together the materials of culture into a life, people are performing acts of meaning – the recomposition of these modes of life and thought requires acts in the discernment of meaning. And I believe that it is also apparent that this discernment of meaning is an achievement, one that is often hard-won. So, it is my fascination with these questions that has powerfully reinforced my interest in the activity of meaning making, and in the structures, frames and circumstances that facilitate this.

Some twenty years ago this interest in the discernment of meaning took me to the work of Gregory Bateson (1972, 1979), who described two principal mechanisms at work in this achievement. He proposed that all responses in the 'world of the living' are founded on the drawing of distinctions around contrasting descriptions of the experiences of life – according to Bateson, it is this 'double description' that provides a basis for the drawing of distinctions in the world, that establishes conditions for the discernment of meaning. Bateson also described the conditions that were required to establish, in people's minds, a receiving context for 'news of difference'. This receiving context was a network of presuppositions that provided a frame for the receipt of news of difference, one that would render this news sensible or comprehensible. Bateson often referred to these receiving frames as 'restraints of redundancy', and, according to him, it was these restraints that made it possible for people to respond selectively to their experiences of the world – for people to 'pluck the new from the random'. I have always understood the network of presuppositions that form the basis of these restraints of redundancy to be culturally informed, and the meanings that these restraints give to the events of the world to be carriers of culture.

More recently, considerations that are aroused by these questions have taken me to the work of Jacques Derrida (1978) who, like Bateson, proposes a relational understanding of all meanings. In focussing on texts, Derrida strongly challenged the idea of 'presence' – that is, the idea that meanings inhere in whatever it is that is being described and are 'present' within people's consciousness – and asserted that all descriptions are arrived at through a process of discernment. In his textual analyses, Derrida sought to demonstrate that all description is achieved in response to other contrasting descriptions that are absent from but implicit in the text. Although I have not considered people's lives to be texts, I do believe people's expressions of living to be based on a foundation of discernment, which is a meaning-making achievement. And I have explored ways in which these absent but implicit descriptions might be excavated through the deconstruction or unpacking of the stories of people's lives (White 2000).

While the ideas of Bateson and Derrida provide some account of how people assemble their lives out of 'materials lying about in the society' through the activity of meaning making, it is those propositions about the centrality of the structure of narrative in this achievement that have more significantly shaped my explorations. According to these propositions, it is narrative structures that provide people with the receiving frames that make it possible for them to attribute meaning to the events of the world – the structure of narrative provides a principal frame of intelligibility through which people engage in the activity of making sense of their experiences of life. In structures of narrative, events are linked together in unfolding sequences through time according to a theme or a plot. These structures also provide the basis for people to derive a range of conclusions about what these events might say about their own intentional states, and the intentional states of others – including purposes, values, beliefs, hopes, dreams, and commitments in life. The mind of folk psychology is invoked by these means. These structures of narrative, and the specific narratives that are formed in the context of these, are not strictly determining of the meanings that people give to their experiences of life. Rather, they contribute to conditions of indeterminacy[8] within determinacy (White 1991). This indeterminacy within determinacy provides a vexing and challenging conundrum.

> *The extent to which persons are self-interpretive – they are not passive in their response to lived experience, but active in ascribing meaning to this – leads us to a second consideration of the significance of agency and the subject in the constitutionalist account of identity ... As the interpretation of experience according to narrative is an achievement, then so is identity. There are always contingencies thrown up in life for which a*

> *person's dominant self narrative is not tailor-made. These must be managed. As well, there are many gaps in personal narratives. Such gaps are the outcome of the degree to which ambiguity and uncertainty feature in all stories. In the living of, or in the performance of, self-narrative, these gaps must be filled. And there are always dilemmas to be resolved in the performance of self-narrative: dilemmas that arise from the extent to which inconsistencies and contradictions are a feature of all stories.* (White 1992, p.41)

To summarise, to propose life to be a direct reproduction of the knowledges and practices of culture excludes considerations of how these knowledges and practices find their ways into people's minds and into their expressions of life, of how it is that people pull the materials of culture together to form an identity and a life, and of the processes by which these cultural knowledges and practices are reworked in people's expressions of living. To propose life to be a direct reproduction of culture renders invisible the specific achievement of meaning-making, along with a range of experiences associated with this. This includes the complexities of the social negotiations that provide the basis of this achievement, as well as all of the personal exertions, compromises, struggles and dilemmas associated with the production of meaning.

Narrative as a vehicle of culture

I have briefly reviewed some considerations relating to the activity of meaning making, to the structure of narrative, and to the constituting role of cultural knowledges and practices. I have proposed that in this constituting role, these knowledges and practices are not strictly determining of life. It is my understanding that the narratives of people's lives are not radically constructed – not derived in a social, cultural and political vacuum – but are shaped by these knowledges and practices that are cultural and historical. It is also my understanding that these narratives are carriers of culture – they are a vehicle for these knowledges and practices. Embedded in these narratives are knowledges of life that sponsor particular ways of living, and that are associated with specific practices of relationship and techniques of self formation.

This understanding of narrative as a cultural vehicle is featured in therapeutic conversations that are unpacking of the stories of people's lives and identities. Not only does this unpacking contribute to the deconstruction of the negative identity conclusions associated with these stories, but it also renders more visible the modes of life and thought that are carried in them – that is, through the unpacking of the stories of people's lives, the extent to which these are the bearers of historical and cultural ways of being in the world and thinking about the world becomes more explicitly known. These therapeutic practices bring the world into therapy in the sense that many routine and unquestioned understandings about life and ways of living become visible as cultural and historical products, and these are no longer accepted as certainties about life or truths about human nature and identity. In this way, what might be termed 'the politics of people's experiences' are made visible and contestable.

The understanding of narrative as a cultural vehicle is also featured in the re-authoring conversations of narrative therapy. In these conversations people do not radically construct alternative stories of their lives and claims about their identities. The alternative identity claims and stories of life that are derived in these conversations are the bearers of other ways of being in the world, and other ways of thinking about the world, that are also cultural and historical. On account of this consideration, these re-authoring conversations are not just about drawing out the alternative stories of people's lives. In addition they also provide a context for the identification of and the rich description of the knowledges of life and practices of living that are associated with these stories. Thus, it is not just those therapeutic conversations that are unpacking of the stories of people's lives and identities that bring the world into therapy. Re-authoring conversations achieve this as well.

This appreciation of the cultural and historical character of these other knowledges and practices has the effect of expanding therapeutic inquiry into the broader realms of living, providing people with new possibilities for drawing on and seeing through culture and history in their efforts to address their predicaments and their concerns. This gives people a basis for the development of some familiarity with ways of thinking and with practices of relationship that were previously little known, for options in self-formation previously unseen, and for the recognition of problem-solving skills not previously acknowledged or available.

The following account of my meetings with Larry and his family provides an example of the sort of possibilities that can become available when the cultural and historical aspects of the alternative stories of people's lives are considered.

Larry and his family

I am meeting with Larry and his parents, Imelda and Eric. I am hearing that Larry, now thirteen years of age, has been a longstanding source of concern to his parents. He has also been a source of concern to the police, to his school teachers and to the parents of other children. Imelda and Eric are particularly worried about Larry's frequent tantrums, his general aggression, and his risky actions. He has already come to the attention of several social service agencies, and has at times been considered 'uncontrollable'. From all accounts Larry has been unmoved by the many efforts so far initiated to encourage him to reform his ways.

Imelda and Eric decided to seek further consultation following a recent crisis. In a 'fit of anger' Larry had held a knife to his mother's throat. This was the 'last straw' for Imelda. In response, she packed her bags and left the family home, vowing never to go back. She stayed with a cousin for a couple of days, and then returned, stating that she would give things one last try. Consulting me was part of the terms of this one last try.

In the early part of my consultation with this family I heard about how angry Larry gets towards his mother, and I learn that it is not at all unusual for him to threaten her at these times. In response to this I seek information about the specificity of his actions when angry:

M: Okay, so I am hearing about how angry you get towards your mother. I'm curious. Do you ever get this angry towards your father?

Larry: Yeah.

M: Would you say more angry, less angry, or about the same?

Larry: Same.

M: So, have you ever held a knife to your father's throat?

Eric: [shakes his head]

Larry: No.

M: Would you ever consider it?

Larry: No

Eric: [shakes his head]

The fact that Larry would raise a knife to his mother's throat when angry with her but not follow suit with his father when angry with him had me speculating about the gender politics expressed in his actions. It is not unusual for sons to advocate for the power relations of gender in their interactions with their mothers. On account of this speculation, I was curious to know about Eric's position on Larry's actions:

M: Larry, do you know what your father thought about this?

Larry: What?

M: What he thought about you holding a knife to your mother. Was he for it or against it?

Eric: [takes a quick breath, registering surprise at my question]

Larry: Against it I s'pose.

M: How did you know that?

Larry: [shrugs his shoulders] Just do.

M: [to Eric] Is that right?

Eric: I am surprised you would ask this question. Of course I was against it!

M: [to Imelda] Is this something that you would have known? That Eric was against this?

Imelda: Of course I did. I wouldn't have stayed if I hadn't known this.

M: Have you always known this about Eric, that he would be opposed to Larry threatening you?

Imelda: Eric isn't always that tuned in to what is happening, and we have had words about this. But in the end I do get his attention, and he's always been respectful.

M: [to Eric] Is this something that you would relate to?

Eric: Yeah. Imelda's right about this. It is true that I have let her down at times, but I feel I have done my best to respect her as woman. It's a principle with me.

M: Is your respect here specific, or is it a general principle in your interactions with women?

Eric: I would like to believe that it is general. What do you think Imelda?

Imelda: Yeah. I reckon it is a general thing. He doesn't treat women bad.

M: [to Eric] I guess that you have witnessed men's disrespect of women.

Eric: Sure have. Why, even at work there has been some harassment. I never want any part of it. I won't join in.

M: Does anyone in your workplace know how you feel about this? Would anyone there know what your position is on this?

Eric: [shrugs] I guess so.

M: Right now I am curious about what has provided you with a foundation for this principle of respect, about how you have managed to hang on to this, and about whether you have found this difficult at times. I was also curious to know about what hanging onto this says about the sort of values and beliefs that might be important to you. What are your thoughts about this?

It was with this question that I initiated a line of enquiry that I hoped would provide a framework for Eric to more richly describe these other ways of being for men in relation to women. However, despite the fact that Eric was clearly interested in these questions, his responses were quite sparse. In the context of our conversation, the knowledges and practices associated with these ways of being remained thinly known. But I did learn that Eric's father, Kevin, would have also disapproved of Larry's threatening of his mother, and that he would support what Eric had been saying about respect.

Larry's abusive actions towards Imelda had been the focal point of our initial conversation, and I had a strong appreciation of the importance of Larry assuming full responsibility for these actions. However, while such considerations about a person's responsibility for perpetrating abusive actions are paramount, so too are considerations about who might best assume responsibility for addressing such actions – about whom it might be appropriate to engage in acts of redress. And this is a different consideration. It was my understanding that Larry's abusive actions were shaped by knowledges that contribute to a particular constructions of men's and women's identities, and by practices of power that are associated with these knowledges. I did not believe that Larry was a primary author of these knowledges and practices – they are out there, at large, in our communities. On account of this, I believed that it would not be appropriate for me to establish a context in which it was required of Larry that he take sole responsibility for initiating acts of redress. Rather, as these knowledges and practices have been developed and finely honed in men's culture, I believed that in these circumstances it would be more appropriate for a community of men to join with Larry in this initiative.

It was with these considerations in mind that I began to ask questions about Larry's evident surprise at much that he was now hearing from Eric. The responses to these questions determined that Larry was open to further explorations of men's ways of being in relation to women, and the option of a separate meeting with Larry, Eric, and Kevin was suggested. The purpose of this meeting would be to put Larry more in touch with his father and grandfather's position on matters of men's relationships with women, to generate some proposals for steps that Larry might take to mend what might be mended, and to assist Larry in explorations of other ways of being in the world as a young man. As part of the plan, if Larry wished he could invite another young man to the meeting to be a support person for him (he eventually chose his cousin, Peter), and it was agreed that all proposals arising from the meeting would be taken back to Imelda to give feedback on. Eric liked the idea, and thought that Kevin would be more than happy to play this part. Larry said that this was okay by him because 'it takes the heat off'. Imelda was very relieved to hear this plan, as, for so long, she 'had born the brunt of responsibility for stopping Larry's abuse'. This meeting took place two weeks later, and the following transcript is taken from a point mid-way through:

M: So, Kevin, that is how your name came up. Eric implicated you in his ability to resist these disrespectful ways of relating to women. Does this strike a chord for you? Do you have a sense that you might have contributed to such a foundation? Or are you surprised to hear this?

Kevin: Well, I can't recall it ever being discussed, but I do strongly believe that women are to be respected, and I haven't liked what Larry says and does at times. [turning to Larry] You know that, don't you son? [turning back to me] But I don't know how much it is okay for me to interfere.

M: Eric, you talked with me about your father's respect of women. From what you have seen, how does that translate into action? What does your father do that is a demonstration of this respect?

Eric: Well, he does listen to women. He doesn't put down their ideas, and he doesn't raise his voice when he disagrees with my mother, or when he is feeling frustrated. And I have seen him frustrated.

M: What has this meant to you?

Eric: Well, I guess he has been a good example for me in lot's of ways.

M: [turning to Kevin] What is it like for you to hear this?

Kevin: A bit of a surprise really!

M: What is it like for you to be implicated in Eric's actions in this way?

Kevin: Well, let me see. I've also got lots of shortcomings. But I would have to say that it is pleasing, because we all want a good life for everybody. It isn't anything that I really knew, because it is nothing that we have talked about. To be honest, I would also have to say that this is something that I probably don't think about enough.

M: [addressing Kevin and Eric] Would you now have a go at talking to Larry about two things. First, would you have a go at catching him up on what this says about what you both value and what you believe, and on your understandings about what responsibilities are to be honoured in men's relation-ships with women. And second, would you have a go at catching him up on your ideas about how this can be put into practice in men's relationships with women. This second point is important. It is one thing to know something, it is another thing to have the skills to act on this knowledge.

Kevin: That's a lot. But we will give it a try.

Eric: Yeah, we could do that.

M: And maybe I could help to break it up a bit by asking you some more questions as we go along?

Eric: Yeah. That would definitely help a lot.

Over the course of the ensuing conversation, other ways of being for men in relation to women were drawn out. This included knowledges that differently shape gender constructions, and, as well, a range of practical examples about how to put these knowledges to work. At points during this conversation I encouraged Larry and his cousin, Peter, to engage in a retelling of what they were hearing. It was apparent that both Larry and Peter were genuinely surprised over much of this, and by what it was that Eric and Kevin were respecting in each other. At this juncture, I introduced some questions about the broader contexts of these ways of being as men:

M: Kevin, I would like to know about how you got introduced to these ways of being a man in relation to women. Would it be okay with you if I asked some questions about this?

Kevin: Fine, fine. Go ahead. Maybe I'll learn a few things [chuckles].

M: Earlier in our conversation Eric was telling me that you can make yourself available to things that are hard for you to hear. When you think of this ability, who else do you think of ?

Kevin: Let me see now. The first thing that comes to mind is an uncle of mine who was a youth leader in a boys' club when I was young. He had a position of authority, and I remember some of the blokes that were in this position were pretty strong about the correct line, like little dictators. But my uncle wasn't like this. You could still have an opinion around him. And he could cope with hearing things that were hard to hear. Everyone just knew this about him. And I can remember him taking advice from my aunt. Which, I know now, at the time, I know wasn't that usual [meaning that it was unusual to witness men in these positions taking advice from their women partners].

M: Do you know how he achieved this?

Kevin: Never asked him. But it might have had to do with the fact that he came from a family with a 'background'.

M: A background?

Kevin: Well, his family was different. I remember something about Quakers, but don't have a lot of details.

M: Did your father have this background too?

Kevin: No, when it comes to patience and understanding, he wasn't too flash. This uncle was his brother-in-law.

M: [turning to Eric and Larry] Did you know this about Kevin's uncle?

Eric: No way.

M: What about you Larry?

Larry: Nope

M: Peter?

Peter: Me neither.

M: Kevin, could you tell us some stories about your uncle. I would like to know what you saw in his actions. This way we might get some clearer ideas about what he thought about things, and about how he went about things. For example, about what he knew to do in responding to what was difficult. About what he knew about respecting women. And about the ways that he held himself open to other people's opinions when these other people weren't male friends, or men with authority.

Kevin: Sure, let's do it.

In the ensuing conversation, many particularities of the knowledges and practices of living that characterised this uncle's ways of being were described.

I met with Kevin, Eric, Larry and Peter on two further occasions, and then on three more occasions with Eric, Larry and Imelda, pursuing further this inquiry into alternative ways of being for men in relation to women. In these meetings, these ways of being became more richly known to all of the members of this family, and it became evident that these were becoming more influential in guiding Larry's actions. It was also evident that Eric was becoming more proactive in addressing some of the gender politics expressed in his workplace. Imelda happily provided feedback on a range of proposals for how Larry might respond to her in a variety of circumstances, including those in which he experienced frustration, and on proposals for the steps that he might take to mend what might be mended in his relationship with her.

It was established that any future concerns about Larry's relationship with Imelda could be referred back to this committee of men who would take the responsibility of joining with him in the development of further proposals for addressing these concerns, and of supporting him in initiating actions based on these proposals. I would be available to join this committee of men if this was found to be necessary. It wasn't. Subsequently, on two occasions when Larry was having difficulty in figuring out how to respond to Imelda's concerns, the committee was reconvened, and a range of options caucused on. Larry experienced no difficulties in taking up some of those options deemed most appropriate.

In this work with Larry and his family, I understood the claims about Eric's preferred ways of being in the world as a man to be associated with knowledges of life and practices of relationship that were cultural and historical. This consideration shaped an inquiry that provided a basis for the development of a familiarity with ways of thinking and with practices of relationship that were previously little known, of options in self-formation previously unseen, and for the recognition of problem-solving skills not previously acknowledged or relatively available.

Summary

At the outset of this paper I proposed that the familiarity that people have with narrative inquiry, and their responsiveness to this inquiry, has to do with the fact that many of the practices of this inquiry are closely linked to a particular tradition of understanding life and identity that is deeply historical. Following Bruner (1990), I referred to this tradition as 'folk psychology'. This is a tradition of understanding that is distinguished by the notions of personal agency and intentional states, and is one that was displaced over the period of the development of the modern psychologies.

This folk psychological tradition of understanding life and identity was reinstated in the social sciences in the 1960s and 1970s, particularly through the 'interpretive turn' in cultural anthropology. This reinstatement of folk psychology was accompanied by renewed interest in the activity of making meaning, and in the structures of narrative. This activity and these structures are the primary focus of many of the practices of narrative therapy that bring forth the mind of folk psychology.

In clarifying some of the proposals for therapeutic practice that are shaped by this tradition of folk psychology, I discussed the production of 'multi-intentioned' lives, of 'joined' lives, of 'multiple authenticities', and of 'inhabited' lives. I then discussed some of the implications of the acknowledgement that personal and community narratives are historical and cultural products, and the carriers of specific knowledges of life and practices of living that shape people's ways of being in the world.

At different points in this paper I included transcripts of therapeutic conversations along with brief summaries of my conversations with Paul in regard to the unpacking of 'unresolved issues'; with Jill's family in relation to rendering her suicide sensible; with Ricky about his relationship with trust; and with Larry and his family over addressing the power relations of gender. Through the inclusion of these stories it was my intention to illustrate some of the ways in which the practices of narrative therapy are shaped by notions of personal agency and intentional states, and, on account of this, strongly linked to a particular historical tradition of human understanding referred to as 'folk psychology'.

Acknowledgement

I would like to thank David Epston for his helpful comments on an earlier draft of this paper.

Notes

1. For a fuller account of the constituents of folk psychology, see Jerome Bruner's *Acts of Meaning* (1990).

2. I have a longstanding interest in Foucault's (1973, 1979) analysis of the significance of this development in the shaping of modern psychological understandings and practices. According to this analysis, in the context of this normalising judgment, people are assigned a precise location in relation to norms about life that are chiefly constructed in the modern disciplines. This normalising judgement also provides certain incitements for people to operate on their own lives in specific ways in order to close the gap between these assigned locations and these norms. In as much as this assignment of a precise location in relation to these norms is cellularising or individualising of life, the introduction of the idea of internal states that shape human expression contributes to the sub-cellularisation of life. According to this analysis of modern power, the sub-cellularisation of life that is achieved through the construction of internal states contributes yet further to mechanisms of social control. This sub-cellularisation provides further opportunities for people to engage in the normalising judgement of their own and each others' lives. And it has the effect of inciting people to operate on their own and each others' lives in efforts to reproduce the psychological norms that have been constructed through the history of the professional disciplines.

3. In contrasting internal and intentional states I am following Jerome Bruner (1990). Other contrasts work equally well. For example there are the essentialist/non essentialist, structuralist/non structuralist, and the naturalistic/constitutionalist distinctions.

4. The Jamesian tradition was displaced following Freud's Clark University lectures in 1908. It is interesting to speculate as Beels (2001) does on what would have happened to the early twentieth century's psychologies if this had not occurred and had not captured the professional and public imagination.

5. Jerome Bruner (1990), a figure who contributed significantly to this cognitive revolution, provides an interesting account of this history and the outcome of this development.

6. For discussion of this definitional ceremony metaphor and of its relevance to therapeutic practice, see White (1995, 1997, 1999).

7. Over the past two decades David Epston and I have explored many possibilities for recruiting audiences to the preferred developments of people's lives. We have never considered these explorations to be peripheral to our consultations. Rather we have viewed them as highly significant to the authentication of the identity claims associated with these preferred developments, and to the endurance of these developments. Engaging with the work of the cultural anthropologist Barbara Myerhoff (1982, 1986) in the latter part of the 1980s contributed further to our understanding of the processes associated with the audience's contribution to the authentication of the preferred developments and identity claims of people's lives (for example, see White & Epston 1989). Our acquaintance with Barbara Myerhoff's notion of the definitional ceremony also contributed to further developments and refinements in what we came to call (following Myerhoff) 'outsider-witness' practices. These retellings are invariably quite transformative in their effects.

8. I have borrowed this term and its sense from Wolfgang Iser (1978) and Jerome Bruner (1986).

References

Bateson, G. 1972: *Steps to an Ecology of Mind.* New York: Ballantine.

Bateson, G. 1979: *Mind and Nature: A necessary unity.* New York: Dutton.

Beels, C. 2001: *A Different Story: The rise of narrative in psychotherapy.* Phoenix, Arizona: Zeig, Tucker & Theissen.

Bruner, J. 1986: *Actual Minds, Possible Worlds.* Cambridge, MA: Harvard University Press.

Bruner, J. 1990: *Acts of Meaning.* Cambridge, Mass: Harvard University Press.

Clifford, J. 1988: *The Predicament of Culture: Twentieth century ethnography, literature and art.* Cambridge, Mass: Harvard University Press.

Derrida, J. 1978: *Writing and Difference.* Chicago: University of Chicago Press.

Foucault. M. 1973: *The Birth of the Clinic: An archaeology of medical perception.* London: Tavistock.

Foucault, M. 1979: *Discipline and Punish: The birth of the prison.* Middlesex: Peregrine Books.

Foucault, M. 1980: *Power/Knowledge: Selected interviews and other writings*. New York: Pantheon Books.

Geertz, C. 1973: *The Interpretation of Cultures*. New York: Basic Books.

Geertz, C. 1983: *Local Knowledge: Further essays on interpretive anthropology*. New York: Basic Books.

Geertz, C. 2000: *Available Light: Anthropological reflections on philosophical topics*. New Jersey: Princeton University Press.

Gergen, M.M. & Gergen, K.J. 1984: 'The social construction of narrative accounts.' In Gergen, K.J. & Gergen, M.M. (eds): *Historical Social Psychology*. Hillsdale: Lawrence Erlbaum Assoc.

Iser, W. 1978: *The Act of Reading*. Baltimore, MD: John Hopkins University Press.

James, W. 1890: *Principles of Psychology*, Vol.I and II. New York: Holt.

James, W. 1892: *Psychology: Brief course*. London: Macmillan.

James, W. 1902: *Varieties of Religious Experience*. New York: Longmans.

Meares, R. 2000: *Intimacy and Alienation: Memory, trauma and personal being*. London: Routledge.

Myerhoff, B. 1982: 'Life history among the elderly: Performance, visibility and remembering.' In Ruby, J. (ed): *A Crack in The Mirror: Reflexive perspectives in anthropology*. Philadelphia: University of Pennsylvania Press.

Myerhoff, B. 1986: 'Life not death in Venice: Its second life.' In Turner, V. & Bruner, E. (eds): *The Anthropology of Experience*. Chicago: University of Illinois Press.

Rosaldo, M. 1984: 'Toward an anthropology of self and feeling.' In Shweder, R.A. & Le Vine, R.A. (eds): *Culture Theory: Essays on mind, self, and emotion*. Cambridge: Cambridge University Press.

Rosaldo, R. 1993: *Culture and Truth: The remaking of social analysis*. Boston: Beacon Press.

Spence, D. 1982: *Narrative Truth and Historical Truth: Meaning and interpretation in psychoanalysis*. New York: Norton.

Turner, V. & Bruner, E. (eds) 1986: *The Anthropology of Experience*. Chicago: University of Illinois Press

White, M. 1991: 'Deconstruction and therapy.' *Dulwich Centre Newsletter*, No.3. Reprinted in Epston, D. & White, M. 1992: *Experience, Contradiction, Narrative & Imagination: Selected papers of David Epston & Michael White, 1989-1991*.

Adelaide: Dulwich Centre Publications. Reprinted in Gilligan, S. (ed) 1993: *Therapeutic Conversations*. New York: W.W.Norton.

White, M. 1992: 'Men's culture, the men's movement, and the constitution of men's lives.' *Dulwich Centre Newsletter*, Nos.3&4. Reprinted in McLean, C., Carey, M. & White, C. (eds) 1993: *Men's Ways of Being*. Boulder: Westview Press.

White, M. 1995: 'Reflecting teamwork as definitional ceremony.' In White, M.: *Re-Authoring Lives*. Adelaide: Dulwich Centre Publications.

White, M. 1997: 'Definitional ceremony.' In White, M.: *Narratives of Therapists' Lives*. Adelaide: Dulwich Centre Publications.

White, M. 1999: 'Reflecting-team work as definitional ceremony revisited.' *Gecko*, Vol.2. Reprinted in White, M. 2000: *Reflections on Narrative Practice*. Adelaide: Dulwich Centre Publications.

White, M. 2000: 'Re-engaging with history: The absent but implicit.' In White, M.: *Reflections on Narrative Practice: Essays & interviews*. Adelaide: Dulwich Centre Publications.

White, M. & Epston, D. 1989: *Literate Means to Therapeutic Ends*. Adelaide: Dulwich Centre Publications. Republished as White, M. & Epston, D. 1990: *Narrative Means to Therapeutic Ends*. New York: W.W.Norton.

chapter four

Narrative practice and the unpacking of identity conclusions

Daniel*

Daniel, a sad looking boy of eleven years of age, was brought to see me by his parents, Tom and Lucy, who were at their wits' end. They complained that their lives were being destroyed by Daniel. According to them, he was 'bringing trouble down' on their lives in every way imaginable. He had been expelled from two schools, and was now suspended from a third. He was in trouble with the police, with neighbours, with the parents of his peers, and, as well, was creating havoc at home. As I listened to these details, it was clear to me that Lucy and Tom were attributing very sinister motives to Daniel's actions. In fact their account of these events was laced with a range of highly negative conclusions about Daniel's identity, and these were painful for me to hear. Amongst other things, they had concluded that 'he was out to destroy the family', that he was a 'worthless good-for-nothing', 'useless to himself and everyone else', and a 'dead loss when it came to efforts to do anything for him'. Daniel's response to all of this seemed one of studied indifference. He just sat there, neither confirming nor protesting this account of his life and identity. But I had the sense that he felt himself to be at one with these very negative conclusions.

I said that on hearing these details I was developing some appreciation of just how frustrating the situation must be. Tom responded to this, exclaiming: 'And you don't even know the half of it yet!' My response: 'Would it be okay then if I asked some questions that would assist me to more fully understand the effects of all of this trouble on your lives?' Lucy and Tom gave me the go ahead, and before long I was learning that this trouble had painted a highly negative picture of Lucy's identity as a mother, one that had made it very difficult for her to have connections with other mothers around the subject of parenting. On account of this, it had been quite isolating of her. I also learned that this trouble had negatively affected her relationship with Daniel, blocking what she would otherwise have to give to her son. 'What is it like for you that this trouble has so powerfully influenced your picture of yourself as a mother?', I asked Lucy. And, 'How do you feel about the extent to which all this trouble has come between you and Daniel?' In response to these questions, Lucy became quite tearful.

* All names are pseudonyms.

I asked what the tears were all about, and Lucy began to tell me about her deep sadness over what she was missing out on as a mother, and about what she felt cheated of in not knowing her son as she might.

Turning to Tom, I asked about what he would say about the most significant effects of this trouble on his life. He was at first nonplussed by my question. He said that he hardly knew where to start. So I asked him about in which ways this trouble had specifically affected his sense of being Daniel's father. Tom responded that he had never been able to get onto the map in terms of being a father to Daniel – Daniel had never allowed him to assume such a place. 'Is this state of affairs okay with you Tom?', I asked. His response was one of part resignation and part despair: 'Oh, I had my dreams, but what is the point'. I was soon interviewing Tom about these dreams, which we together traced all the way back to the point of Daniel's conception. After a time, I asked: 'So what would you say all of this trouble has done to those dreams'. His emotionally laden response was: 'It has crushed them'.

It was now time to turn to Daniel. 'Would it be okay with you', I asked Tom and Lucy, 'if I now consulted Daniel about the effects of all of this trouble on his life?' 'Go ahead', Lucy said, 'but I doubt that you will get much out of him'. 'Daniel', I said, 'As you have heard, I've just been having a talk with your mum and dad about how all of this trouble has been affecting their lives. Now I would like to ask you some similar questions. Would that be okay?' In response, Daniel shrugged his shoulders. I decided to proceed: 'What has this trouble been talking you into about yourself? What sort of picture has it been painting of you?' Daniel's response to this was to again shrug his shoulders. I said: 'Would it be okay if I was to assume that this shrug meant that it was alright for me to proceed with my questions, and that you will let me know if this isn't the case?' I thought I detected a slight nod. Although I wasn't sure of this, I decided to proceed on this basis of this impression: 'Would it be okay by you if I asked your mum and dad for their thoughts on this?' Another shrug. 'Thanks. I will assume that you are giving me the go ahead, unless you tell me otherwise', I said with some enthusiasm, sensing a degree of collaboration from Daniel.

Upon consulting Lucy and Tom about this question, Lucy said that she thought that this trouble was painting a pretty dismal picture of who Daniel was. Tom elaborated on this, saying that he thought that this trouble was talking

Daniel into the idea that he was 'a lazy good for nothing', a 'waste of time as a person', and 'even that he was useless'. These descriptions were the very ones that Tom and Lucy were giving at the outset of our meeting, but they were no longer being collapsed onto Daniel's personhood. These descriptions had been deprived of their authority to characterise Daniel.

What a journey we had been on! At the outset of the interview Tom and Lucy had shared with me a number of highly negative identity conclusions that they and others held about Daniel, and I had suspected that Daniel was secretly in agreement with this appraisal of who he was and of what his life was about – that he believed that these conclusions spoke of the truth of his identity, that he felt at one with these. Now, thirty or forty minutes later, in this conversation, we were experiencing the development of some shared sense that these conclusions didn't speak to the totality of who Daniel was, and that he also had an identity that was somehow separate from, and that even contradicted, these negative conclusions. These negative conclusions no longer represented the truth of who he was.

This opened the door for our work together to become more collaborative. 'Daniel, what is it like for you to be talked into such negative things about yourself?' This time Daniel was shrugless in his response. He glanced at his parents, and, taking this as a cue, I asked them: 'What do you think it is like for Daniel to be talked into such negative ideas about who he is?' In response, Tom said, 'I guess that it makes him lonely – and miserable too'. 'I reckon that he is secretly sad about this', said Lucy, 'because I am sure that the wet patches that I sometimes see on his pillow in the mornings are from tears'. I looked at Daniel, wondering whether or not he would confirm this. Suddenly I saw a tear surfacing in the corner of his eye. We all saw it. Daniel turned his head aside, his tear evaporators working overtime. When he looked back the tear had vanished. But things were never the same after this tear. There was a way forward. The existence of this tear was a signal that Daniel had taken a position on the trouble that everyone else had taken a position on. Now, for what seemed like the first time, there was an opportunity for the members of this family to be joined together, with me, in their efforts to break their lives from what had become such a terrible predicament.

Unpacking negative identity conclusions

Externalising conversations, like the one I have just described, represent just one possibility of many in a range of narrative practices. They are by no means a requirement of narrative therapy and, in fact, externalising conversations are very often absent in my own work with the people who consult me. But they can be very helpful in the unpacking of some of the very negative identity conclusions that people bring with them into therapy.

I am sure that you, the reader, have some familiarity with conclusions of this sort - for example, conclusions that one is 'hopeless', 'a failure', 'incompetent', 'unworthy', 'hateful', 'inadequate', and so on. Perhaps you have had some first-hand experiences of such identity conclusions at some time in your own life, even if this has only been to momentarily entertain a sense of failure to be a real therapist when things haven't been working out quite in the way that you hoped they would! This wouldn't surprise me. After all, the sense of personal failure has never been more freely available to us, and has never been more willingly dispensed as it is in these contemporary times. When these negative identity conclusions are more enduring, people experience them to be quite capturing of their lives. Such conclusions are often found to be paralysing of action in regard to the predicaments of people's lives, and can contribute to a strong sense of one's life being held in suspense, of one's life being frozen in time.

Often when describing and demonstrating the utility of externalising conversations, I have illustrated the extent to which these conversations can contribute to the unpacking of people's negative identity conclusions – which I often refer to as thin conclusions (after Geertz's thin description [1973]). In fact, I believe that one of the primary achievements of externalising conversations is this unpacking of the thin conclusions that people have about their own and about each other's identity. In this activity, these conclusions are deprived of the truth status that has been assigned to them – these conclusions cease to carry the authority that they did. I believe that this outcome is readily apparent in the externalising conversation that I had with Daniel and his parents. Perhaps another brief example will serve to further demonstrate the utility of these conversations in depriving these thin conclusions of their truth status:

Jane was referred to me with a diagnosis of borderline personality disorder. The psychiatry resident, Sarah, who made the referral, was hoping that there was something more that could be done to assist Jane to interrupt the cycle of admissions to hospital. This was a cycle that was fuelled by episodes of cutting, by suicide gestures, and by depression. Early in my conversation with Jane and Sarah, I discovered that Jane believed herself to be a hateful person, and that she hated herself on account of this. In response, and with Jane's permission, I began to interview her and Sarah about the influence of self-hate in her life. This interview was shaped by questions like:

- *What is this self-hate talking you into about yourself?*
- *What seeds is it planting in your mind about who you are?*
- *How does it have you treating your own body?*
- *Does it invite you to nurture your body, or does it require you to reject your body?*
- *Does it have you treating your body with compassion, or does it encourage you to take a hierarchical and disciplinary approach to your body?*
- *What does it want for your connections with other people?*
- *Does this self-hate set itself up as an authority on other people's motives towards you?*
- *How does it do this, and how does this affect your relationships with others?*
- *Would it be okay if I asked some questions to get the low down on how self-hate speaks, and on the forces that support self-hate?*

These and other questions took us into an extended externalising conversation that had the effect of depriving hatefulness of the truth status it had for so long maintained. This first step in our work together was profoundly significant in its contribution to Jane eventually breaking free of the cycle of hospital admissions, to the discovery of her passion for justice, and to her wider engagement with life.

In summary, in here describing and illustrating the utility of externalising conversations, I have given an account of the extent to which these provide a mechanism for the unpacking of negative and disabling identity conclusions. But this isn't all that I have emphasised when the subject is externalising conversations.

Re-authoring conversations

I have also drawn attention to the part that these externalising conversations play in opening space for yet other conversations, ones that contribute to the generation of more positive identity conclusions. And more than this, these other conversations, that at times I refer to as 're-authoring conversations' (for example, see White 1992, 1995), also contribute to the identification of and to the exploration of the very knowledges of life and practices of living that are associated with these positive identity conclusions. It is in this way that these re-authoring conversations (that externalising conversations often make way for) contribute to the thick or rich description of people's lives and of their relationships. This thick or rich description of lives and relationships is generative of a wide range of possibilities for action in the world that were not previously visible. It is in these re-authoring conversations that people step into other experiences of their identity. These re-authoring conversations are actually shaping of, or constituting of, life and identity. To illustrate this point, I will return briefly to the story of Daniel.

Our externalising conversation made way for the expression of alternative identity claims on behalf of all family members. These claims contradicted those associated with the problem-saturated story of their lives. These identity claims were implicit in Lucy's distress about what the trouble had been talking her into about herself as a mother, and in her lament about the extent to which trouble was interfering in what she would otherwise have to express in her relationship with Daniel. Alternative claims about who Tom was as a man and a potential father were implicit in his expressions of despair over his crushed dreams. And alternative identity claims about Daniel were present in Lucy and Tom's account of what the trouble had been talking everyone into about his character, and, as well, in his extraordinary tear.

In subsequent conversations, all of the dreams, hopes, purposes, values and commitments that were expressed in these alternative identity claims were drawn out. Amongst other things, the history of Tom's dreams about fatherhood were traced further back to a pledge he had made with himself at the age of fourteen during some very tough times, a pledge that he had never previously spoken of to Lucy or to Daniel. This was a pledge not to do to any future son of his what was being done to him by his own father. Lucy had the opportunity to speak of the connection between the mothering of Daniel and some of the significant purposes and values of her life, and to identify those figures of her history that she was linked to in these. She also provided an account of the initiatives that she had taken in her relationship with Daniel that were a reflection of these purposes and values, which were powerfully acknowledged in the context of our conversations. Daniel, with assistance from Lucy and Tom, began to put words to his tear. These included a previously unacknowledged longing for 'friendship' with his parents and others.

As our conversations evolved, the knowledges of life and practices of living associated with these dreams, pledges, purposes, values and longings were richly described. This provided options for all family members to take initiatives in their relationships with each other, initiatives that hadn't previously been available to them. As an outcome of this, trouble ceased to be a significant presence in the lives of these three people.

In summary, I have emphasised and illustrated the potential of externalising conversations to (a) assist people to break from negative identity conclusions, and to (b) pave the way for the introduction of other conversations which contribute to the exploration of and generation of more positive identity conclusions. These positive identity conclusions are not stand-alone phenomena. They are associated with specific knowledges of life and practices of living. On many occasions, upon initial inquiry, these other knowledges and practices are only evident in very thin traces. However, it is my understanding that these knowledges and practices have the potential to significantly shape other ways of being in the world, and other ways of thinking about life. Therefore, if these knowledges and practices can become more richly described throughout the process of therapeutic conversations, then previously unimagined possibilities for action become available to the people who consult us.

I believe the rich description of these other knowledges and practices to be a vital consideration. For the purposes of emphasising this, I will mention the work that I do with men who are referred to me for perpetrating abuse. Amongst other things, the focus of initial conversations is on opening space for these men to take some preliminary steps in assuming responsibility for the abuses that they have perpetrated, and on the development of some understanding of the short-term and potential long-term effects of these abuses on the lives of others. These initial conversations also focus on the deconstruction of the identity conclusions that shape a sense of male supremacy and entitlement, and on the ways of being in life and thinking about life that are associated with these conclusions. But this is not the end of the story – in fact, it is barely the beginning.

I don't have the assumption that providing these men with an opportunity to challenge these 'truths' about identity, and the ways of being in and thinking about life, that are associated with these truths, is sufficient. I do not hold an assumption that this makes it possible for these men to spontaneously step into more understanding and non-abusive ways of life that are the product of some 'intrinsic' knowledge. Rather, what I understand to be crucially important at this time is to assist these men to engage in extended explorations of other knowledges of life and practices of living that are associated with some of the new identity claims that these men arrive at in these conversations. In this way the particularities of other territories of these men's lives are drawn out, and they finally have another place to stand that is outside of those familiar territories which feature abusive ways of being. I believe that it is only with these more extended explorations of other knowledges and practices of living that a significant and enduring sense of personal responsibility can be embraced.

Naturalistic accounts of life and identity

I hope that I have succeeded in introducing a couple of the key aspects of externalising conversations: how they can assist people to break from negative identity conclusions and how they can open space for further re-authoring conversations which involve the rich description of other knowledges of life and practices of living. I now wish to devote some space to clarifying some misunderstandings which commonly occur in relation to these conversations.

One misunderstanding concerns the idea that the positive identity claims that are richly described in this work are somehow representative of the 'truth' of the identity of the persons concerned – the development of these positive identity claims is regularly taken into modern humanist understandings of life. This misunderstanding persists despite the care that I have taken, in what I have written and taught about narrative practices, to emphasise the historical and cultural basis of all identity claims.

Another misunderstanding concerns the alternative knowledges and practices of living that are identified in re-authoring conversations. These are often taken to be the 'true' knowledges and the 'genuine' or 'authentic' practices of life, that are considered to be 'intrinsic' or 'unconscious' in nature. However, I have never considered this to be the case. Rather, I have always assumed these knowledges and practices, that shape other ways of going about life, to be the products of history and culture. They have been constructed in and developed in the contexts of the many institutions of culture, including the institution of the family – be that family of origin, family of imposition, or family of choice.

It is in the context of these misunderstandings that narrative practices are portrayed as 'libratory' practices that are considered to be freeing of people to live a life that is more accurately a reflection of their 'true nature', of their 'essential humanness', and of their 'authenticity'. I believe that this humanist take on narrative therapy is quite understandable, because, in contemporary western culture, humanist discourses have become pervasive in the shaping of our taken-for-granted understandings of most expressions of life. These understandings provide naturalistic accounts of life and identity. In them, identity is taken to be the product of nature, of human nature; a nature made up of 'essences' or 'elements' that are to be 'found' at the centre of who one is. According to this take on life and identity, the problems that people experience are the outcome of forces that are oppressive of, repressive of, or distorting of the essences or elements of human nature. The solution to people's problems that is proposed by these naturalistic notions is to identify, to challenge, and to throw off these oppressive, repressive and distorting forces so that people might have the opportunity to become more truly who they really are, so that they might be free to live a life that is a more accurate reflection of their human nature. According to this version of things, although people's problems can be understood in historical terms – that problems develop over time in the course of people's lives – the account of the solution is on the outside of history. It is a naturalistic account.

Deconstructing naturalistic accounts of life and identity

Now, what is this thing 'human nature'? One thing that is clear is that it hasn't always existed. Another thing that is clear is that, in the history of the concept of human nature, it has not always been the same thing – what are considered to be the primary essences and elements of human nature change from era to era. Here

I will briefly review how human nature has been cast in contemporary western culture. For the purposes of this article, in this review I will restrict my focus to those accounts of human nature that emphasise essences or elements that are considered to be personal properties, and that are routinely referred to as 'resources' and 'strengths'.

If I was to ask you, the readers of this paper, whether or not you possessed any personal properties like strengths and resources, it is my guess that a great many of you would respond in the affirmative: 'Why, of course I have these things'. And if I was to ask you whether these personal properties are relevant to your identity, it is my guess that many of you would again respond in the affirmative: 'Of course. But isn't this true for everyone? These are the building blocks of people's identity'. The existence of these elements or essences of a 'self' that we call strengths and resources is now mostly a taken-for-granted fact. But these essentialist ideas about identity are relatively novel ideas, not just in the history of the world's cultures, but also novel in the history of western culture.

Perhaps some cultural comparison might illustrate this point about the novelty of these ideas in the history of the world's cultures:

I am sitting with a group of elders from several Indigenous Australian communities in the Western Desert area of Australia. I am there with a couple of Aboriginal people with whom I regularly work in partnership, and we are discussing, through an interpreter, an assignment we have been invited to step into by these elders. This assignment has to do with addressing some very significant and pressing predicaments and concerns about developments within their communities, all of which relate to the effects of the invasion and occupation of their country by Europeans over two hundred years ago. In this discussion, I learn about many of the initiatives that have already been taken by these elders to address these predicaments and concerns. They had engaged in these initiatives in circumstances that were highly discouraging them.

I am in awe of these initiatives, and would like to find a way of acknowledging this. My efforts to find ways of acknowledging this awe are shaped by my knowledge of the fact that traditional Aboriginal culture is non-essentialist in its understandings of life and identity. This knowledge is important, for what do you think would be the outcome of me reflecting on what these initiatives said to me about the personal strengths and resources of these elders? Probably, under the circumstances, this would be met with silence in the context of our campfire meeting. However, if there had already been the development of some trust in our connections, I predict that the response of these elders might have been a not-so-polite version of:

> *Why don't you keep that Euro-centred psychological claptrap to yourself? Do you have to colonise our understandings of life as well as everything else. When you understand us in these ways you disrespect our ancestors, who are walking beside us and holding our hands, and who make this work possible. And you are disqualifying the Dreaming.*

So, although I am sure that most of us unquestioningly affirm the presence of these elements or essences and consider them to be universal phenomena, the possession of personal strengths and resources is not a general global phenomenon. The peoples of many other cultures still do not understand their lives in these ways. Apart from this, these essences and elements of human nature haven't been around for all that long even in mainstream western culture.

The possession of personal properties has been a growing general phenomenon of western culture for several centuries, one that received a considerable boost with the development of the modern liberal theory that provides much of the foundation of the western democratic state. Modern liberal theory enshrines the individual's right to the ownership of private property, and to the exclusive use of and disposal of anything that might be gleaned from this property. An individual may cultivate his/her property to improve one's assets, or mine it in order to capitalise on one's resources. Along with the individual's possession of land that was legitimated in modern liberal theory, was an associated sense of the individual possession of their own identity as a property. It was understood that the self was a manifestation of an internal property, held by individuals, and that this was what gave individuals the ability to use their external property to improve its assets or to garner its resources. This idea of self as a manifestation of specific properties served to legitimate the individual's possession of the fruits of their labour.

In understanding identity as constituted by properties that are owned by individuals, people came to possess themselves. In this possession of the self, it became possible for one to cultivate one's properties to improve one's assets, to mine one's properties in order to capitalise on one's resources, and so on. These days we experience encouragement from every direction to take possession of ourselves, to engage in the internal farming of our lives through self-cultivation, and to take up internal mining enterprises that have us digging deep to get in touch with our personal resources, and to excavate these resources so that they might be brought to the surface, put into circulation and capitalised on.

I would like to emphasise that in here speaking of the humanist re-interpretation of narrative practices as I have, and of the development of identity as personal property in which can be found elements and essences of a self that are frequently referred to as strengths and resources, it is not my purpose to suggest that these are 'wrong', 'bad' or 'unhelpful' ideas. In speaking of these notions about human nature as I have, it is not my intention to be dishonouring of any ideas held precious by whomever might be reading this article. And in unpacking these humanist understandings in the way that I have, it is not my intention to discredit the many significant achievements of humanism. Further, in speaking of these naturalistic or essentialist understandings of life and identity in the way that I have, I am not suggesting that we can totally free ourselves from, or even that we should attempt to avoid in everyday life, trafficking in these understandings when the cultural context of our lives is contemporary western culture. Rather, it has been my purpose to emphasise the fact that:

a) these essentialist or naturalistic ideas that today shape our taken-for-granted understandings of life and identity came to the centre stage of western culture in relatively recent history,

b) human nature has not always been what it now is considered to be, and whatever it is considered to be is always a product of history and culture,

c) we have not always had identities that are our personal property, nor have we always possessed these essences and elements that are usually referred to as strengths and resources, and that

d) in taking an opportunity to deconstruct these naturalistic accounts of identity and life, we don't have to be so tied to the unquestioned reproduction of them in our lives and in our work with others.

In this article, I have restricted my focus to the deconstruction of naturalistic accounts of identity that are taken to be personal property. However, because there are so many naturalistic accounts of identity available to us today that we didn't have in recent history, there seems to be unlimited scope for the deconstruction of the 'things' of modern identity, even the things of relationship identity. For example, take 'relationship dynamics'. None of us have had these things for very long. Relationship dynamics are a development of recent history, and they have become increasingly popular over the past three decades. In fact, this is so much the case that there can now be no question about the general success of relationship dynamics. These days more and more people are having them, and I wouldn't be surprised if many of the readers of this paper have experienced the development of these in their own relationships.

However, despite the success of relationship dynamics, we can ask the question: 'Is it a good idea to have relationship dynamics?' In raising this question, I am not suggesting that people didn't used to have troubles in their relationships, and even misery, prior to the onset of relationship dynamics in the 1960s. And I am not taking a general position for or against the construct of relationship dynamics. But in raising this question we have the opportunity to address other questions[1].

- At what point did these ideas about relationship dynamics come to centre stage in our understandings of relationship?
- What were the historical circumstances that gave rise to these?
- To what use have these ideas been put?
- What did these ideas make possible?
- And what are the limitations and hazards associated with this notion of relationship dynamics?

We could ask the same questions about psychological needs, although they have been around a little longer. We first started having these things in the late 1920s and early 1930s. But it's been in the past four decades that psychological needs have really taken off – the recent historical landscape is dotted with huge outbreaks of these things. These days everybody routinely experiences psychological needs, and understands much of what they do in relation to them.

Limitations and hazards of naturalistic accounts of life and identity

In the following discussion I will draw out what I understand to be some of the limitations and hazards associated with naturalistic accounts of life and identity within the context of therapeutic conversations. But before doing so, I want to acknowledge some of the many valuable contributions of humanism in both the micro- and macro-contexts of life. For example, the idea that one's identity is one's own property, in which can be discovered certain essences or elements of human nature, has been put to work in ways that are challenging of acts of domination and exploitation. For a person to claim to own one's voice can be a powerful strategy in the face of the imposition, by others, of authoritative and negative accounts of one's identity. In this strategy, one truth claim, that is deeply historical and cultural, is employed in acts that are challenging of and refusing of other truth claims that are being imposed by others. And there is a great wealth of examples of the ways in which humanist and liberation philosophies have been put to extraordinary uses within the context of significant social movements.

So then, why, if I can acknowledge many humanist achievements, am I interested in deconstructing popular identity claims that are based on naturalistic accounts of life? This is principally because I believe that in the specific context of therapeutic conversations there are a number of limitations and hazards associated with these naturalistic accounts, and that these invariably outweigh the possibilities associated with these notions. I believe that when alternative identity claims, along with their associated knowledges of life and practices of living, are understood to be representative of people's human nature, options within therapeutic conversations are significantly limited. One foremost concern that I have in regard to this is that if people's preferred identity conclusions are assigned a naturalistic status, and if therapeutic conversations are cast as libratory, this will very significantly reduce the options for therapists to take responsibility for what it is that is being constructed in the name of therapy. And more than this. If the outcome of these conversations is understood to be an expression of human nature or of that which is authentically true about people's lives, it becomes very difficult for therapists to embrace any ethical responsibility for the real effects of their conversations with the people who consult them. Another concern, that

I have already addressed in this article, has to do with the extent to which these naturalistic accounts close options for the rich description of the knowledges of life and the skills of living that are associated with the preferred identity conclusions that are generated in therapeutic conversations.

I will here briefly review just some of the other limitations and hazards that I believe naturalistic accounts of life pose in the context of therapeutic conversations:

1. First, in reading human expression as a surface manifestation of certain elements and essences that are of one's own nature, these naturalistic understandings tie us firmly to the reproduction of the cherished 'single- voiced' individualities that are a hallmark of western culture – these are the encapsulated and relatively isolated individualities that I am sure readers will be familiar with. In reproducing these single-voiced individualities, these naturalistic accounts of life and identity can shut the door on opportunities for people to engage with more multi-voiced experiences of identity. These are experiences in which the voices of some of the significant figures of one's life become more present when it comes to matters of one's identity (see White 1997).

2. Second, these naturalistic accounts of identity construct powerful global or universal norms about life, norms that emphasise notions of 'wholeness', of 'self-possession' and of 'self-containment'. In reproducing these global norms within the context of therapeutic conversations, therapists are implicated as agents in the operations of modern forms of social control. These are forms of social control that are based on the normalising judgement of people's lives. This normalising judgement encourages people to further their efforts in the policing of their own lives in order to close the gap between where they stand in the various continuums of health and development and these culturally constructed norms.

3. Third, these naturalistic accounts of life and identity are intimately related to the modern phenomenon of the production of weaknesses and deficits, and of the disorders and the pathologies. For example, those discourses that contribute to an understanding of identity by evoking elements and essences of a human nature, like strengths and resources, are at one with the discourses that contribute to an understanding of identity by evoking the idea of

weaknesses and deficits – people would not understand their difficulties in life as expressions of weaknesses and deficits if there were no strengths and resources. And therapists would not understand people's expressions in terms of pathologies and disorders if it wasn't for the contrasts provided by naturalistic accounts of life.

4. Fourth, there is the potential for naturalistic accounts of identity to shape understandings that are marginalising of others: 'We managed to get through what others don't survive on account of our personal strengths and resources'. In marginalising others in this way, these naturalistic accounts obscure the contexts of people's lives, including the politics of their experience. This includes conditions of disadvantage that deprive people of the opportunities and material conditions that would make it possible for them to 'get through'. These naturalistic accounts can also be considered to be marginalising on the basis that they obscure the contribution of the 'other' to whatever it is that is taken to be one's preferred identity conclusions, and to the development of one's knowledges and skills of living.

5. Fifth, naturalistic accounts of people's significant achievements encourage wonder and can be discouraging of curiosity. In the context of therapeutic conversations, such wonder invariably provides a fullstop to wider explorations, whereas curiosity brings with it opportunities for more extended conversations that contribute to an appreciation of complexity. As well, when wonder shapes a therapist's responses to the preferred developments of people's lives, in efforts to acknowledge these developments s/he is vulnerable to reproducing the modern practices of applause that feature judgement – 'giving affirmations', 'pointing out positives', 'providing reinforcements', and varieties of 'congratulatory responses'. This closes the door on options for practices of acknowledgement that feature significant retellings of the stories of people's lives, which are much more effective in contributing to the rich description of their identities.

I have here outlined some of the limitations and hazards associated with naturalistic accounts of the significant developments of people's lives. It is my contention that therapeutic conversations shaped by these accounts powerfully restrict what otherwise might be rich conversations – conversations that attend to the multi-faceted and multi-storied character of all expressions of living. In so doing, many of the alternative territories of people's lives are left unexplored.

Unpacking naturalistic accounts of life and identity

If these naturalistic accounts dead end what otherwise might be rich conversations that attend to the multi-faceted character of all expressions of life, what options are available to therapists when presented with such accounts? One option is to initiate conversations that might be unpacking of these accounts. Just as externalising conversations can unpack people's negative truths of identity, identity conclusions that have been assigned a positive truth status can be taken into conversations that are unpacking of them.

Although processes that are unpacking of naturalistic accounts of identity are not dishonouring or diminishing of treasured understandings, this proposal often presents us with a significant personal challenge. The proposal to unpack our own preferred identity claims can be experienced as an invitation to step onto and to disturb hallowed ground, and at times it is refused on this basis. Facing this challenge can be difficult. It is one that we are often inclined to turn away from and to avoid. The desire to stay comfortable with our familiar and taken-for- granted understandings of life and identity is strong, and it often seems an easier option to proceed to unpack other people's identity conclusions when these are not the one's that we personally favour, and to preserve our own favoured notions by refusing to question these, and by refusing to submit these to conversations that are unpacking of them. But I believe that the refusal of this challenge and the maintenance of this personal comfort can be at a considerable cost – it can contribute to a life lived thinly.

In the context of therapeutic conversations, a decision not to introduce the option of unpacking naturalistic accounts of identity can be very significantly limiting. It can shut the door on a range of opportunities for us to engage the people who consult us in conversations that will contribute to the rich description of their lives and identities. This will exclude a range of potentially exciting explorations of other territories of people's lives, joy-filled engagements with new vistas and horizons of identity, and the sort of delight that is the outcome of experiencing the unexpected in therapeutic conversations. For it is in the unpacking of these naturalistic accounts of identity that we find so much more than we could have expected to find. Apart from this consideration I believe that a decision not to explore this option will lead to our own lives and our own work being thinly experienced.

Unpacking resilience

I am now sitting with Helen. Her agenda for our conversation is to explore yet more possibilities for addressing the effects of the abuses she had been subject to in her childhood and as a young woman. She considered that she had already managed, with the help of others, to turn back much of this, but wanted to go yet further in what she referred to as the reclaiming of her life. In the early part of our conversation I asked Helen for her understanding of what it was that had seen her through what she had been put through, and of what it was that had contributed to her success in turning back many of the effects of these abuses in the way that she had. In response, Helen said that she thought it was her 'resilience' that had made it possible for her to achieve this. I inquired about the history of Helen's awareness of this resilience, about the first naming of it for herself, and about what this discovery had meant to her.

Helen's responses to my questions put me in touch with the profound significance that she attributed to the discovery of the resilience that she had possessed and expressed through the history of her life. This constituted a highly valued identity conclusion. However, as I began to reflect on my understanding of the significance of this discovery, she said: 'But resilience is not enough. If it was, it wouldn't be necessary for me to be meeting with you now'. I suggested that further explorations of this resilience might provide her with some more avenues for addressing the effects of the abuses she had been through, and requested Helen's permission to ask some questions about this. Helen said that this would be fine. Here I will give just a small sample of these questions. I did not ask these in a barrage-like fashion. Instead, these questions were shaped by and sensitively attuned to Helen's responses.

The first set of questions encouraged Helen to richly describe the ways of being and thinking that resilience is an emblem for:

- When this resilience is most present for you, how does it affect what you do?
- How does it shape how you are in life?
- What does it make possible in your relationships with others?
- How does it assist you to go forward in your life?
- How does it affect what you are thinking at these times?

The second set of questions engaged Helen in richly describing her relationship with resilience:

- Do you know how you have been able to maintain a connection with this resilience through all that you have been through?
- Have there been times in your life at which you could have been dispossessed of this connection?
- What steps did you take to maintain this connection?

The third set of questions provided an opportunity for Helen to richly describe what it was that had been sustaining of her resilience:

- Do you have any thoughts about what it was that was sustaining of this resilience over all these years?
- For example, did you bring some hopes to this resilience?
- Could you say a little about what sort of hopes were sustaining of this resilience?
- Do you know how it was that you were not just resigned to what you had been served up in life?
- How did you get introduced to the idea that life could be different for you?

The fourth set of questions engaged Helen in richly describing her discernment of injustice:

- At what point did you first become conscious of the fact that what you were being put through was not okay? Do you know how you achieved this consciousness?
- What is it that this says about your position on justice and injustice?

- Would it be okay for me to ask you some questions about how this position on justice has been expressed in your history?

In response to these questions, Helen developed a rich description of the social skills and of the very knowledges and practices of life that were associated with this notion of resilience; of the skills or know-how that she had developed and put to work in maintaining her relationship with her resilience; of the hopes that had been sustaining of this resilience, and of how she had been introduced to these hopes; and of her position on justice and of the multiplicity of ways that she had taken this up in her own life and on behalf of others. I will provide here a brief example of just one of the avenues of inquiry that were opened by these questions.

In response to questions about how it was that Helen had been introduced to these hopes that her life might be different, she found herself thinking about her class teacher in her second year at high school – Mrs Murphy. Helen had been going through a particularly hard time, and, on account of this, her attention to school work had been minimal and her concentration in class had been poor. To Helen's surprise, Mrs Murphy hadn't been critical of her over this. Instead, she had been highly considerate and patient, and had been quick to show interest in any constructive contributions from Helen – in fact, Mrs Murphy seemed more interested in these contributions than she was in the performance of the top pupils. As Helen was reflecting on these events of her history, she reached a conclusion that Mrs Murphy must have had suspicions about what she was going through. She also had a stronger realisation about the efforts Mrs Murphy had made to befriend her.

This account of events in Helen's second year of high school opened options for conversations about what it was that Mrs Murphy had appreciated about Helen that others were oblivious to, and about how this recognition and acknowledgement may have contributed to Helen getting through what she had. It also opened options for conversations about what Mrs Murphy's actions reflected about the purposes and values that had been important to her in her career as a teacher, and about whether or not Helen's responses to these actions would have been confirming or disconfirming of these purposes and values. As Helen decided that her responses would have been confirming, I encouraged her to speculate about what it might have been like for Mrs Murphy to experience this from her as a young woman of fourteen years of age. The outcome of this very touching and quite emotional conversation was that Helen was able to bring forth Mrs Murphy's presence in her life at times of duress. At these times she now had options for summoning Mrs Murphy's voice on matters of her identity, and this was effective in displacing the voices of those who had perpetrated abuses on her life. When Helen was ready, we located Mrs Murphy, who had retired from teaching, She remembered Helen and was enthusiastic to meet her again and to join our conversations. These conversations were glorious, but that is another story.

Here, I have introduced some of the categories of questions and a brief account of one of the conversations that contributed to a relatively thorough-going unpacking of Helen's resilience. It was through this inquiry and conversations like these that Helen achieved her goal of turning back what she had referred to as the 'remnants' of the effects of the abuses of her life. Helen was right. As she had said: 'Resilience isn't enough'. But resilience unpacked was.

A naturalistic account of resilience as a personal property was not enough, but when resilience was seen as an emblem for a range of alternative identity conclusions as well as knowledges about life and skills of living, when the histories of these were more richly described, and when this inquiry encouraged a significant re-engagement with certain figures of her history, many new options for action became available to Helen. These were options that enabled her to turn back the effects of the abuses of her life.

Finally, I will turn to a story that is illustrative of the possibilities that become available to us, as therapists, in the further development of our practices when we have the opportunity to engage in conversations that are unpacking of naturalistic accounts of our work.

Unpacking intuition

Joe, a therapist from a local agency, decided to consult me for supervision. This decision was made in response to a frustration that he was experiencing in his work. In many of his consultations, things just were not working out in the way that he hoped they would. He wanted to be rid of this sense of frustration, and to have a better time of his work. 'Was this frustration a constant presence?', I asked. 'Mostly' he said, 'although there have been the occasional times when I have been free of it'. I wanted to know how he would account for these times, but Joe found it difficult to define the particularities of this. Eventually he concluded that at these times things seemed to come together for him in almost a fortuitous way, and, if this related to anything that he was doing, it was probably on those occasions that his 'intuitiveness' was present. I inquired about this sense of being intuitive, and discovered that although Joe experienced this to be a highly-prized quality, it was one that was simply too elusive to be relied upon in his day-to-day work.

I wanted to know how things went in Joe's conversations with people when this intuition was present. I heard that at these times he was able to respond in ways in which people 'felt deeply heard and touched', and that these responses seemed to provide a turning point for the people who were consulting him. This was what Joe wanted to experience more of in his work. I asked him if it would be okay for me to ask some questions about his intuition that might be challenging of this notion, but not disrespectful of it. I made it clear that I understood that intuition was something that he treasured, that he may decide not to risk asking questions of it, and that it would be fine should he decide to leave this untouched. I also said that although these questions of intuition were not necessary in order for us to proceed in our work together, the unpacking of this could well be an option that might provide a solution to the frustration that he was having such a difficult time with.

Joe decided to take a chance on this, and invited me to ask some questions of his intuition. So I asked him to catch me up on the circumstances of a recent consultation in which this intuition was featured. He talked about a family that had been consulting him over recent weeks. I interviewed Joe about his experience of intuition in his work with this family, and about his understanding of the family members' responses to his expressions of this. I also interviewed Joe about the events surrounding these expressions. With this information, we then stepped into a conversation that was unpacking of Joe's intuition. This conversation was initiated by a series of questions. I will provide a sample of these here. I did not ask these questions in a barrage-like fashion. Instead, each question was shaped by and sensitively attuned to Joe's previous response.

The first set of questions encouraged Joe to link his therapeutic responses to the invitations offered, by family members, for him to join with them in particular ways:

- *It is my understanding that you experienced this intuition being available to you at a time that your therapeutic responses were being embraced by the people of this family. What awareness do you have of the invitations that had been offered, by family members, for you to join them, in their lives, in the way that you did?*
- *Do you have a sense of which of these invitations you were being most respectful of in your therapeutic responses?*
- *What was it like for you to be invited into these people's lives in this way?*

The second set of questions encouraged Joe to link his expressions to the cues that family members gave about what sort of therapeutic responses would be significant to them. This set of questions also encouraged Joe to provide an account of the skills that he was engaging with that made it possible for him to attend to these cues in the way that he did:

- *This intuition was present at a time when your responses were particularly significant to family members. Do you have any thoughts about what cues they offered about what sort of responses would be significant to them?*
- *Could you provide me with some understanding of how you have developed a sensitivity to such cues? About how you developed these skills in identifying and responding to cues about what therapeutic responses would be more appropriate?*
- *How was this sensitivity expressed in your therapeutic responses?*
- *What can you tell me about some of the contexts of your own life that have provided fertile ground for the development of this sensitivity?*

The third set of questions contributed to the development, on Joe's behalf, of a consciousness of the extent to which some of his therapeutic responses were particularly relevant to the members of this family because they prioritised an agenda that was of shared significance to them all:

- *Intuition was a feature of your work at a time when the people of this family felt that you were honouring of their agenda for the consultation. How did you go about recognising and allocating a priority to an agenda that was of shared significance to the different members of this family?*

- *What thoughts do you have about how you and family members contributed to the negotiation of this shared agenda?*

The fourth set of questions drew Joe's attention to the skills expressed in his 'understanding ways of being' with this family, and that shaped his responses in a manner that was experienced as resonant, by family members, in terms of their understandings of life:

- *It is your sense that this intuition was active when family members felt deeply understood by you, and when you were expressing yourself in ways that seemed to fit well with their familiar understandings of life. What are you aware of in the history of your own personal experience, that may have been taken up in our understanding of the experiences of the members of this family?*
- *Can you think of any other contexts of your life in which you might have become acquainted with, and skilled in, the understanding ways that you expressed here?*
- *And how did these experiences contribute to the shaping of your therapeutic responses in ways that fitted with understandings of life that were familiar to members of this family?*

The fifth set of questions focussed on the identification of some of the general skills and knowledges employed by Joe in the fashioning of his therapeutic responses:

- *Your intuition was reflected to you in the fact that your therapeutic responses made a significant difference to this family. Could I ask you some questions that might assist you to provide an account of the skills or the know-how that shaped your responses, that contributed to them making a difference?*
- *Could you provide me with some account of the knowledges of life that were expressed in your responses?*
- *What thoughts do you have about the historical contexts of your life that have provided a basis for the development of these skills and knowledges?*

In response to these and other similar questions, Joe developed a rich description of the skills and knowledges that he was engaging with in his work with this family – skills and knowledges for which intuition was an emblem. And in identifying many of the contexts of his life that provided fertile ground for the generation, acquisition, and refinement of these knowledges and skills, he also had an opportunity for a significant re-engagement with his own history. Through this re-engagement with history, the voices of some of the more influential figures of his life were acknowledged, including that of his maternal grandmother, an extraordinary woman who had been a focal point for the working-class community that he grew up in – she had been an unassuming but strong figure who had always been available to support neighbours and friends through times of trouble and desperation, yet never imposed on their lives. In finding new ways of acknowledging the contribution of these figures to his life and work, the voices of these figures were more present for Joe in his ongoing therapeutic explorations.

In subsequent conversations with Joe, there were yet further opportunities to unpack intuition. Within the context of therapeutic conversations, there are many options available to us to render more visible the contributions of the 'other' to preferred therapeutic developments and to preferred therapist identity conclusions – that is, to render more visible the contributions made to these developments and identity conclusions by the people who consult therapists. In the example given above, these contributions included the family-member initiated cues and the invitations that had been extended to Joe, which had been identified and acknowledged in our earlier conversations. Following this, we had further conversations in which we extended our understandings of the contribution of this family to what it was that Joe had identified as intuition.

Such contributions are invariably significant, yet rarely acknowledged. People who consult therapists often go to some lengths in persevering with their therapists through thick and thin. In these efforts, these people are often very understanding of therapists when they lose the plot, are quick to validate therapists when they are on track, and are encouraging and supportive of those therapist responses that strike a chord for them. As well, many of the conversations had with people touch therapists in ways that are sustaining of them in their own lives and in their work with others. When these contributions can be identified and acknowledged in the course of therapeutic conversations, people become aware of options for furthering their partnerships with the therapists they are consulting. In these circumstances, therapists are less likely to experience a sense of burden, and more likely to find their work invigorating.

With the unpacking of intuition, which was for Joe a preferred identity conclusion, and with the rich description of many of the knowledges and skills that this intuition was an emblem for, the frustration that had been so troublesome to Joe dissipated. What had been relatively intangible – intuition – was now something tangible that could be known in its more intimate particularities. These skills and knowledges were now more available to Joe to reproduce in his work with other people seeking consultation, and he began to have a uniformly better time of this work.

Conclusion

In this paper I have described a number of aspects of narrative practice. In the story of Daniel and his family and of the preliminary steps taken to establish a shared position in relation to trouble, and in the story of Jane breaking from self-hate, I have presented accounts of the ways in which externalising conversations can assist in the unpacking of people's negative identity conclusions. I have also addressed the importance of an appreciation of the fact that the unpacking of these conclusions is not enough. Alternative knowledges of life and practices of living, that in the first place are often only visible as faint traces, must be more richly described in order to create new possibilities for action and life. These other knowledges and practices can be understood in various ways. I have proposed that naturalistic accounts of these knowledges and practices, that interpret these as expressions of essences and elements of a 'human nature', are relatively new understandings of life, and that these are culturally and historically specific understandings. Further, I have suggested that, within the context of therapeutic conversations, these naturalistic accounts bring with them particular hazards and limitations that tend to outweigh the possibilities associated with them.

In the retellings of the story of Helen and of the unpacking of resilience, and the story of Joe and of the unpacking of intuition, I have described some of the options that become available for therapeutic conversations when we move beyond naturalistic accounts and into the realms of history, culture and family. It is through this unpacking of these naturalistic accounts that we come to know the history of alternative knowledges of life and practices of living. It is through this unpacking that we come to know how people's lives are linked to the lives of others around shared themes and values. It is through this unpacking that we can engage with the unexpected. This, I believe, can make all the difference.

Note

1. The questions that I provide here are Foucauldian.

References

Geertz, C. 1973: 'Thick description: Toward an interpretive theory of culture.' In Geertz, C.: *The Interpretation of Cultures*. New York: Basic Books.

White, M. 1992: 'Deconstruction and therapy.' In Epston, D. & White, M.: *Experience, Contradiction, Narrative and Imagination*. Adelaide: Dulwich Centre Publications.

White, M. 1995: *Re-Authoring Lives: Interviews and essays*. Adelaide: Dulwich Centre Publications.

White, M. 1997: *Narratives of Therapists' Lives*. Adelaide: Dulwich Centre Publications.

chapter five

Addressing personal failure

Introduction

The phenomenon of personal failure has grown exponentially over recent decades. Never before has the sense of being a failure to be an adequate person been so freely available to people, and never before has it been so willingly and routinely dispensed. This paper describes therapeutic options relevant to addressing this sense of personal failure. It also describes the operations of modern power, for it is the rise of a distinctly modern version of power that is associated with the dramatic growth of failure. Offering a map to guide therapeutic explorations in this area, and interspersed with transcripts of therapeutic conversations, this paper then concludes with a 'failure conversations exercise' to assist in the development of practice skills.

Part One

Modern power and the production of failure

Narrative therapy is at times taken to be a 'solution oriented' therapy, perhaps because the practices of narrative therapy provide people with new approaches to the predicaments of their lives. However, the definition 'solution oriented' is inadequate in that it doesn't take in many of the narrative practices that do significantly focus on people's problems. This attention to people's problems is evident in much of what has been written and taught on the subject of narrative therapy. Take, for example, externalising conversations, which introduce people to new explorations of the problems of their lives. It is in the context of these explorations that problems that people find to be at the centre of their lives and identities, and which have often asserted a massive presence, are dramatically decentred, and significantly attenuated or dissolved. Externalising conversations have now been applied to a wide range of purposes, including to those that assist people to situate their problems in the political, cultural, and socio/economic contexts of their lives.

As part of my longstanding interest in, and inquiry into, people's problems, I have been vitally interested in the phenomenon of personal failure. This interest in personal failure has importantly shaped my therapeutic practice, and has been strongly emphasised in my teaching and in some of my writings over the past fifteen years or so (e.g. White 1987, 1995a). In speaking of the phenomenon of personal failure, I am not referring to people's failure to complete the routine tasks of everyday life: for example, to negligent action when care is required (for instance, in the nurture and protection of young children), or to incompetent action when precision is required (for instance, in the driving of a car or in the piloting of an aircraft). Rather, I am referring to those actions that are routinely taken to reflect on people's identity in ways that construct them as failures by definition: a personal failure in regard to making it in life; in regard to reproducing a life that is a reflection of the cherished norms for what it means to be a 'real' person; in regard to adequately engaging in the favoured identity projects of contemporary culture.

I believe that the phenomenon of personal failure has grown exponentially over recent decades. Never before has the sense of being a failure to be an adequate person been so freely available to people, and never before has it been so willingly and routinely dispensed. It would now be very rare for me to meet a person in the course of my practice, in the course of my teaching, or in the course of my everyday social life, who hasn't experienced, at different times and to different degrees, the spectre of personal failure (here I am talking about a sense of inadequacy, incompetence, insufficiency, deficit, backwardness, and so on) looming large in their lives.

In this paper it is my intention to more fully describe therapeutic options relevant to addressing this sense of personal failure. Before describing these options, I will here briefly comment on what I believe to be a significant factor in the development of this phenomenon – that is, the operations of modern power. For it is the rise of a distinctly modern version of power that is associated with the dramatic growth of failure.

Considerations of power

For the past fifteen or so years I have had a strong interest in the analysis of modern systems of power. In this interest I have drawn principally on the work of Michel Foucault (1973,1979,1980,1984), a French historian of systems of thought. Over this time I have explored a range of implications of this analysis of modern power for therapeutic practice, and have in places described some of these explorations (e.g. White 1988/89, 1991; White & Epston 1989).

When considerations of power are raised in the context of therapeutic explorations, invariably it is a classical analysis of traditional power that is evoked. This conceives of a power that is appropriated by certain individuals and groups; of a power that is taken up by these individuals and groups according to particular and unitary interests. This is a power that is understood to exist at a defined centre, and that is exercised from the top-down by those who have a monopoly on it. It is a power that is characterised as principally negative in its function; that is, it is a power that operates to oppress, repress, limit, prohibit, impose, and to coerce. This is a power that people are mostly subject to, not one that people generally participate in the exercise of. In contemporary times this version of power is often considered to be synonymous with the 'system' ('it's the system') that virtually everyone is on the outside of. In situating their lives, people routinely claim a position that is exterior to this power, regardless of whatever privilege they might have on account of where their lives are located in the domains of class, race, economics, and social advantage.

Foucault drew attention to the development of another version of power that exists in the shadows of these traditional operations of power. According to his studies, this is a distinct mechanism of modern power that has, over the last three hundred or so years, progressively displaced many of the operations of traditional power in the contemporary era of western culture. This modern power has now become the predominant system of power in the achievement of social control. This is a power that recruits people's active participation in the fashioning of their own lives, their relationships, and their identities, according to the constructed norms of culture – we are both a consequence of this power, and a vehicle for it. By this account, this is a system of power that is particularly insidious and pervasive. It is a power that is everywhere to be perceived in its local operations, in our intimate lives and relationships. Foucault sought to illustrate the many ways that we live our lives on the inside of the web of power relations of this system of modern power, and to draw attention to the extent to which we have become its unwitting instruments.

Foucault put considerable effort into tracing the history of the development of modern power. I do not intend to provide a summary of this here, but will emphasise that:

a) the operations of modern power were derived through the uptake of self- and relationship-forming practices that were first developed at the local level of culture – in monasteries, clinics, schools, and families, and that

b) over the history of the professional disciplines, criminology, medicine/psychiatry, psychology and social work have played a key role in the further development of the technology of modern power.[1]

On account of Foucault's observations about the pervasive and insidious nature of modern power, he has been considered by some to be a philosopher of despair. However, upon first reading Foucault on modern power, I experienced a special joy. This joy was due in part to his ability to unsettle what is taken-for-granted and routinely accepted, and to render the familiar newly strange and exotic. Apart from other things, I found that this opened up new avenues of inquiry into the context of many of the problems and predicaments for which people routinely seek therapy. But this joy was also significantly due to the conclusions that I formed as I read Foucault's work, and that were confirmed in my readings of his later reflections on the implications of his analysis of modern power. I will list a few of these conclusions here:

a) If systems of power are very rarely ever total in their effects, and if the operations of this modern power are everywhere to be perceived, then examples of opposition to the relations of modern power, or of actions that represent a refusal of its requirements, will be ever present. It is through the analysis of the operations of modern power that this opposition might be rendered more visible and richly known, acknowledged and, under certain circumstances, celebrated.

b) If the operations of modern power are dependent upon people's active participation as its instruments, then, despite the pervasiveness and effectiveness of modern power, it is fragile in a way that traditional structures of power are not. On account of this criterion of active participation, individuals are uniquely placed to challenge and to subvert the operations of modern power. In challenging the dispositions and habits of life that are fashioned by modern power, people can play a part in denying this power its conditions of possibility.

c) If the operations of modern power are derived through the uptake of self and relationship practices that are first developed at the local level of culture, and if they principally operate at these levels – in clinics, schools, families, and so on – then there is the ever present potential for people to contribute to social change through the local development and sponsorship of self- and relationship-forming practices that do not directly reproduce the constructed norms of contemporary culture.

d) If the professional disciplines have played a key role in the phenomenon of modern power, then the culture of therapy is positioned in the heartland of the development of its technology. This conclusion emphasises the small 'p' political aspects of therapeutic practice, and inspires us to work on the development of practices that are 'counter' to this technology when many of the problems that people present to therapists are derived through the operations of modern power.

On account of conclusions like these, this analysis of modern power presents many options for action in relation to the operations of power, options that can be considered small 'p' political. So many expressions of life that might represent acts of opposition to the operations of modern power, or a refusal of its requirements, that would be inconsequential within the context of a classical analysis of power, become substantial. In the context of therapeutic practice, the appreciation of the significance of these expressions of life is invigorating of therapeutic inquiry.

If we are restricted to a classical analysis of power, many of the social forces that are significantly shaping of people's lives and relationships, and of our interaction with the people who consult us, remain invisible. As well as this, the range of options for action in relation to power is significantly narrowed. In the context of this classical analysis, apart from processes of appeal that are ratified in the constitutions and statutes of the institutions of our society, general social dissent, organised resistance, and heroic acts of individual protest, little is deemed relevant as effective action in relation to power. And such action is likely to have little impression on the operations of modern power, which will remain concealed, and therefore relatively unassailable.

Because of this, I believe that to depend on a classical analysis for the understanding of all operations of power can have the potential to contribute to a paralysis of will. This paralysis of will is in part an outcome of the significant frustration that is often experienced in response to efforts to precipitate social reform. This is a frustration that is associated with the finding that many of the acts of opposition that are relevant to a classical analysis of power do not appear to change 'the system'. This paralysis of will is also the outcome of conclusions about the magnitude of the task of achieving social reform, and is evident in the modern sentiment: 'Nothing can be changed without dismantling the system, and, given our position on the outside of the system, this would be an overwhelming and impossible task', and, 'Since we do not have access to the corridors of power, in our efforts to challenge its operations we are reduced to banging our head on the wall'. To depend upon a classical analysis for an understanding of all operations of power often leads to the development of a liberal critique of the status quo, but at the same time fosters a sense of powerlessness to act on this critique. The apparently growing phenomenon of 'neo-liberal fatalism'[2] amongst health/welfare/counselling academics and workers can considered to be, in part, an outcome of this.

The emphasis given in this article to the importance of Foucault's analysis of modern power is not to suggest that a classical analysis of power is not relevant to modern times. It is not to suggest that all expressions of power in contemporary western culture are modern in character. And it is not to suggest that the traditional forms of opposition to the operation of traditional structures of power are no longer relevant as a force for social change. No doubt there are today many operations of power that are institutionalised and that do resemble the characteristics of the classical analysis of power reviewed here – operations of power that appear predominantly prohibitive, oppressive, repressive, limiting, and coercive in their effects. For example, there are those operations of power that are present in race relations and in the subjugation of indigenous people, in gender relations and in the oppression of women, and in the power relations of heterosexism and the disqualification and marginalisation of gay, lesbian, bisexual, and transgendered identities.

On account of this, traditional forms of opposition to the operations of power that are identified through a classical analysis will remain important and relevant to therapeutic contexts. However, in these contemporary times, even many of the operations of what are regarded to be institutionalised power relations depend to a considerable extent on the fashioning of identities through relations of power that are not accounted for by this classical understanding of power. These operations of power that are fashioning of contemporary identities are of modern power.

How power is conceived of largely determines the options that are available to oppose its operations. This article introduces one such option that is founded on the analysis of modern power and that is relevant to therapeutic conversations. I will begin to describe this option by providing an account of my conversations with Max, who was referred to me for supervision.

Max

Max was referred to me by Helen, his supervisor at a counselling agency. He had been employed in this agency for eleven months, and although he was considered to be diligent in the way that he applied himself to his responsibilities, in Helen's view he wasn't living up to his potential. In her opinion, this was clearly evident in his expressions of apprehension about his counselling work, in his general lack of confidence, and in what she presumed to be his low self-esteem.

In addition to this, Helen was concerned that Max was often quite withdrawn in staff contexts, not demonstrating a level of assertiveness considered appropriate to his position. Despite this, she valued him highly. Upon hearing from Max that he thought he might not be cut out for a career as a counsellor, Helen had become concerned that he might be lost by her agency, and to the counselling profession more generally. She had then decided that his difficulties were such that an outside of agency referral for supervision was warranted. Max had agreed to this.

At the outset of my first meeting with Max, he confirmed his supervisors concerns, stating that he also had become increasingly frustrated by his apprehension and general lack of confidence. He had been feeling quite inadequate and had a strong sense of personal and professional failure in relation to this. Although he now thought that he would never make the grade, he had agreed to see me in the hope that there were still some stones to be turned in his efforts to make it as a counsellor and as a more confident person.

Max: So, that's the score. And I don't know where to go from here. I am now thinking that I am not really cut out for this. I have been feeling really inadequate. In fact it's worse than that, I have been feeling quite a failure. I have even come very close to resigning on at least three occasions. So, there you are Michael. Now you have it. What do I do?

M: You said that you had reached a conclusion that you were personally inadequate, and that you feel like a failure. What is it that you feel inadequate in relation to? What is your sense about what you have failed to achieve?

---

* All names are pseudonyms.

Max: It's really about the fact that I feel that I haven't measured up for this counselling position. I want to make it clear that I don't have an argument with any of my supervisor's opinions about me. If I were in Helen's shoes, I'd do the same thing. I would have the same opinion of me. What she has said about my lack of confidence at work, it's true, and I don't think that I am going to be able to make it.

M: Make what? What is it that you are not going to make?

Max: You know. Getting my act together as a counsellor! Like being more assertive! Like achieving some confidence! Like getting adequate and coping with the things that I need to cope with in my work! Like taking things in my stride in a job that surely isn't so hard after all.

M: I get the sense that you feel at the wrong end of everything. Instead of adequacy, you've got inadequacy. Instead of confidence, you've got apprehension. Instead of assertiveness, you've got passivity. Instead of self-assurance, you've got insecurity. Is that how it is?

Max: That's exactly it! I couldn't have said it better!

M: Well, you have been saying it pretty well. You also said that you have been trying to make it as a counsellor in the agency. In finding yourself falling short of the mark, what have you been doing? What have you been doing in your pursuit of adequacy?

Max: I have been giving myself a pretty hard time. Really I have. I've tried to get myself up to scratch. I even give myself pep talks every Monday morning. I am constantly working on how I think about myself, conjuring up images of what I could be. Telling myself that in the next interview and in the next staff meeting things will be different. I'm always working on ways that I think about my work. You name it, I do it.

M: Sounds pretty exacting.

Max: Yeah. For sure! It's exhausting! In fact that's an understatement. I get to feel totally wrung out.

M: Has all of this work that you have been putting into measuring up been working? Has it been helping?

Max: What a joke!

M: This leaves me curious about something. You have a sense of not making it, and you are giving yourself such a hard time, but you have kept going, and you haven't quit. You have nearly quit, but you haven't. Have you discovered something that encourages you, that makes it possible for you to keep going? Or is it just that you let up on yourself at times? How do you keep going?

Max: Do you mean do I sometimes have a flash of inspiration, or something? Because if that's what you are looking for then you should be talking to someone else.

M: No, I wasn't thinking of anything dramatic, but just anything that would help me to understand how you keep going. Perhaps it is something quite small.

Max: I don't know. Well … maybe I do let up on myself at times. In fact, yes, now that I think of it, I am sure that I do, but I don't think that's a good thing. Maybe this is what I should be working on. What do you think?

M: I was thinking more about whether you had perhaps found something that gives you some respite from all of the hard work that you are doing on yourself in your efforts to measure up, in your pursuit of adequacy.

Max: Respite?

M: Or relief, or solace. Or maybe something else … I don't know what word would fit for …

Max: Well. Let's see. All I know is that I do mostly appreciate my clients. Maybe this gives me solace, or lets me take a breather at least. Yes, that could be it. Maybe this is what I cling to. That's not good is it.

M: What do you mean?

Max: Well for one thing, what does that say about my boundaries?

M: Who knows? You are asking the wrong person about that. I am not much into 'boundary think' and 'boundary speak'. But this ability to appreciate your clients in the way that you do, what's this got to do with confidence, assertiveness, self-assurance and so on? What's it got to do with all those things that you have been working on?

Max: Nothing much I guess. I don't think there have ever been any questions about my appreciation of my clients.

M: So there are aspects of your work that you can value that are not accounted for in all of these ideas about who you would be in your workplace if you were making it?

Max: I guess so … Well … Yeah. But this is a pretty basic thing, a bottom-line thing, isn't it?

M: What do you do that keeps you in touch with this appreciation of the people who consult you? What steps do you take in this?

Max: I don't know that I have to do anything. It isn't difficult. I am interested in their lives, so I follow up what I get interested in.

M: Anything else you could think of?

Max: I know my clients are in a vulnerable position, and they are exposing their lives to therapists. I know it would be so easy for them to feel hurt and misunderstood. So I do take care.

M: What are you expressing in your interest in the lives of the people who consult you? And in these steps that are shaped by this interest?

Max: It is just how it is. All I can say is … well … it is just how it is. I am not sure if I can … (trails off)

M: If you were to name what is important to you that is a foundation for this interest and these steps, that is one of those bottom-line things, what words would you come up with? Words that would describe what you would feel comfortable about having to answer for in your work?

Max: The only thing that comes to mind is integrity. I would hope that this is a reflection of my integrity. It is important to me that I never lose touch with this, although sometimes I'm not sure if I always manage to hang onto this in the way that I would want to, because … (trails off)

M: Integrity! Now I would like to ask you some questions about what it is that guides you in expressions of this integrity. But this doesn't really fit with the agenda that was set up for our meeting. It would take us away from working on all of these other things: assertiveness, self-assurance, confidence, and so on. It would also take us away from your pursuit of adequacy. Would that be okay?

Max: That's okay. That's just fine. Really fine! Go for it!

As we proceeded to explore what it was that guided Max in his expressions of integrity, he began to describe a system of values and beliefs that he considered both central in and essential to his life. These included the priority that he put on everyone having a fair go, on being entitled to respect, on possessing the right to be heard, and on having the opportunity to make decisions about their own lives.

As Max was drawing out this system of values in response to my questions, I realised that he was acutely aware of the consequences of power imbalances in relationships, and particularly sensitive to issues of marginalisation. Upon inquiring about the contexts of Max's life that had been generative of this awareness and sensitivity, I learned that he was the eldest son of a sole-parent mother who had contended with many pressing circumstances, and who he had witnessed marginalised and disqualified on many occasions. Max's mother had been acutely aware of the politics of her experience, and in response to being marginalised and disqualified she had never been separated from the values that were precious to her. She had talked openly about the importance of this with her children. The exploration of these contexts of the development of Max's concern for others provided an opportunity for him to yet more richly describe the system of values and beliefs that provided a guide to him in his expressions of integrity.

This in turn opened the door for an inquiry into how the management of this integrity according to these values and beliefs was shaping of Max's self-forming activities (in regard to his interaction with his own life) and his relationship-forming activities (in regard to his interaction with the people who consulted him, with other staff members, and with the agency that he worked for). This also opened the door for speculation about how Max's management of this integrity according to these values and beliefs could be more overtly expressed in these agency contexts. The following excerpts of transcript provide an account of the beginnings of this inquiry.

a) Excerpt one: self-forming activities

M: When you are experiencing this integrity, and feeling more or less at one with the values that we have been discussing, what is that like for you? Are you giving yourself a hard time? Or is it different?

Max: No, at those times it is different. I won't say that I am free of doubts at those times, but I do feel .... What do I feel? Let's see. Maybe 'more relaxed with myself' is a good way of putting it.

M: More relaxed with yourself. Would you say this is to do with a different attitude towards yourself? Or maybe ...

Max: Yeah. I would say a different attitude towards myself.

M: Would you say a little more about this.

Max: I think at those times, which are pretty rare, I feel more accepting of myself. I have a softer approach to who I am.

M: I would like to hear more about this softer approach to who you are, and about what you are accepting of at these times. I would also like to know a little about how this softer approach shapes your life. Would this be okay with you?

Max: Sure. Sure.

M: Okay. Tell me, how would you describe how you are treating your own life at this time?

Max: It's like I'm ...

b) Excerpt two: relationship-forming activities (counselling contexts)

M: We've been tracing out the ways in which this integrity and these precious values and beliefs are implicit in much of your work. We've also been talking about how this shapes your relationship with the people who consult you, and about how this might be touching the lives of these people.

Max: Yeah. I have enjoyed talking about this. There is something about talking about this that gives me a sense of relief. It is a bit hard to put it into words.

M: Would you be interested in a conversation about how this integrity and these values might be given a more overt presence in your counselling work?

Max: Sure! Sure I would!

M: You don't sound at all uncertain about this. Would you care to say why?

Max: No. I don't feel uncertain at all. I think because this might give me some new directions to follow up in my counselling.

M: Well, let's go back over what we've learned about the ways that this integrity and these values are implicit in much of your counselling, and about how these shape your relationship with the people who consult you. We could then speculate about appropriate ways of making this more explicitly visible to the people who consult you.

Max: Okay. Sounds good. I don't think that I would ever have thought of … (trails off)

M: Amongst other things, you said that you make efforts not to impose an agenda on the people who consult you, that you try to be aware of anything that you are doing that might be diminishing of them, and that you endeavour to take in feedback from their responses to let you know if you are going off track. How might this sentiment be more openly expressed in these conversations?

Max: Well, let's see. Well, I suppose that I could do more to set the scene.

M: What do you mean? What's an example?

Max: Okay. Let me think for a minute. Well … Yes, I have an example. From the beginning of my meetings with my clients I could tell them that I was apprehensive about the possibility that I could wind up taking the conversation in a direction that wasn't okay for them. And say that at different points I would be checking in with them, asking them for feedback about the direction of our conversation.

M: Anything else come to mind?

Max: I could also acknowledge to them that there was an inequality of power – you know, in the counselling relationship – and that because of this I could accidentally wind up imposing ideas on my clients. I could work out ways to get feedback from them about this as well.

M: Would setting the context like this contribute to you being more or less apprehensive?

Max: (laughs) Less apprehensive. (laughs again)

M: Let's take up some of the other ways that this integrity and these values are implicit in your counselling, and talk about how they could be made more explicit.

Max: That would be interesting, and it would …

c) Excerpt three: relationship-forming activities (with colleagues and with agency)

M: I have enjoyed hearing about the ways in which this integrity and these important values and beliefs are implicitly shaping some of your interactions with colleagues and with the agency. Is there anything about this integrity and these values that would explain what you have been telling me about your inactivity in meeting contexts?

Max: I don't know.

M: What about in these 'case meetings' that you have mentioned? For example, are there any meeting practices that contradict the sort of practices that would be shaped by this integrity and these values?

Max: Well, I suppose there could be. I suppose so. I have certainly felt uncomfortable, that's for sure. But I have been thinking it is just me.

M: If it isn't just you, what might this discomfort be about?

Max: Well, I suppose that the way that we talk about clients when they aren't there to speak for themselves runs against these values.

M: Would you say more about that.

Max: Yeah. It's not really bad you know, and everybody is trying to help. Everyone's got good intentions. But there are ways that we talk about our clients that I'm sure would not be the same if they were present. I also worry about the possibility that we will wind up making decisions about them and for them when they are not there, that they don't have a voice in.

M: What's your guess about how you would be responding in these meetings if this integrity and these values that we have been discussing were more explicitly present for you, and more openly expressed by you?

Max: Let's see. Well, one thing is that I could speak about some of the questions that I have about how clients' lives are spoken about, and about any decisions that are made when they are not present.

M: Other thoughts?

Max: What else? Maybe I could also suggest that if one of the staff members is concerned about a client and wanting to bring this to a case meeting, then they could talk to the client about this concern, and invite the client to call a case meeting.

M: Sounds like an interesting …

Max: Yeah! And the client could be given options about who might attend such a meeting. Yeah, that would fit.

M: Yeah.

Max: Do you know what's strange? I don't know why I hadn't thought of that before.

M: Let's keep going then. What else do you run up against in agency contexts that might contradict the sort of practices that would be shaped by this integrity and these values?

Max: Okay. Well there is this other situation where …

Discussion

Over a period of two months in which we had four meetings, Max successfully abandoned the pursuit of adequacy. In this time his apprehension was progressively unpacked. This was an apprehension that represented a strongly ethical position informed by integrity and by specific values and beliefs that he held precious, and that fitted with what he eventually named as his life's aspiration: 'to achieve a life of goodness'. Max more richly described, and began to put into practice, numerous options for the expression of this apprehension in an unpacked form – these options were based on the proposals that were generated for more overt expressions of this integrity and these values and beliefs. He immediately began to have a much better time of his counselling work. In staff contexts he gradually became more vocal about agency practices, and this was invigorating of him although it did initially contribute to some complications in his relationships with some of his colleagues.

On account of these complications Max chose to invite Helen, his agency supervisor, along to our fifth meeting, which was structured around the tellings and retellings associated with the practices of definitional ceremony (Myerhoff 1982, 1986; White 1995b, 1999). This was also the meeting to which we had invited Max's mother, Loretta. For the first half of this meeting, Helen and Loretta formed an audience to my conversation with Max in which the story of our first four meetings unfolded. In the context of this, Loretta's contribution to Max's relationship with integrity and with specific values and beliefs was powerfully honoured (as was her contribution to recent preferred developments in his counselling practice and in his agency participation). This was deeply moving for Loretta, and when it came time for the audience or 'outsider-witness' retelling, initially she found it very difficult to speak. Helen's retelling was highly acknowledging of these developments in Max's counselling practice and agency participation. In this, she stated that although these developments were not quite the outcomes she had been expecting upon referring Max for supervision, these had nonetheless presented a number of timely and important challenges to what had become unquestioned and routine agency practices. This she valued highly.

At the beginning of our meetings it was Max's sense of impending failure that was at the centre of our conversation. At this time Max was feeling quite overwhelmed by this sense. Although he was engaged in the hot pursuit of adequacy, he felt that he was losing ground in this, and the task that he had embarked upon seemed increasingly daunting to him. He could not see a way forward, and was very close to resignation. It was in the context of therapeutic conversations shaped by an awareness of the operations of modern power that Max was able to abandon this pursuit of adequacy, as well as the desire to reproduce the highly valued norms of 'assertiveness', 'self-assurance', and 'confidence'.

It is not at all uncommon for me to be consulted by people who, like Max, experience the spectre of failure looming large in their lives. On account of this I have taken a strong interest in the phenomenon of failure, and its link to the operations of modern power. I have had many extraordinary conversations with people as an outcome of this interest. When people consult me about personal failure I routinely anticipate exciting expeditions into territories of identity that have been little charted. I also expect that these expeditions will provide people with the opportunity to step into modes of life and thought that will bring new horizons of possibility to their lives.

In this paper I will provide an account of how these expeditions might be structured. But, before doing so, I will draw out the link between the contemporary phenomenon of failure and the rise of 'modern power'.

Failure and modern power

As mentioned in the introduction to this paper, the dramatic growth of the phenomenon of personal failure is associated with the rise of a distinctly modern version of power that establishes an effective system of social control through what can be referred to as 'normalising judgement' (Foucault 1973, 1979, 1980). Whereas traditional systems of power operate through moral judgement (as an outcome of which it is determined that people's actions are either right or wrong, good or bad, moral or immoral) and through structures of coercion, modern systems of power encourage people to actively participate in the judgement of their own and each other's lives according to socially constructed norms (as an outcome of which it is determined that people's actions reflect degrees of inadequacy, abnormality, insufficiency, incompetency, hopelessness, ineffectualness, deficit, imperfection and worthlessness). Whereas traditional power acts through institutionalised moral judgement to prohibit, to limit, to restrict, modern power acts through normalising judgement to constitute life – that is to form lives, to fashion lives, to shape lives, or to manufacture lives that reproduce the constructed norms of contemporary culture. In participating in this normalising judgement, people are active in the policing of their own and each other's lives, and are deeply implicated in the mechanisms of social control that are characteristic of modern power.

The normalising judgement of people's lives has been made possible through the development of a whole new technology of power that employs various schemes and continuums of normality/abnormality, tables of performance, scales for the rating of every human expression imaginable, and formulae for the ranking of persons in relation to each other. This technology of power also includes specific practices of evaluation that have the effect of inserting people's lives into these schemes, continuums, tables, and scales.[3] Although much of this technology was developed by the professional disciplines and exercised according to formal rules, it now shapes a great many of the taken-for-granted informal practices of popular culture that are highly significant in the formation of modern lives and identities (just for a moment reflect on the character of the popular psychology that is ever present in the glossy human interest journals and gossip magazines of contemporary times).

In response to finding their lives being consistently inserted into precise locations in a range of continuums, tables and scales, people are induced to work to close the gap between these locations and the ideals for personhood that are produced by socially constructed norms. People are induced to actively participate in the judgement of their own and each other's lives according to these ideals. These ideals for personhood are represented by all of those contemporary norms about what it means to be a 'real' or 'authentic' person.

It is through these now routine and culture-wide practices of normalising judgement that the sense of failure has become one of the experiences of personal identity most easily had in contemporary times.

Table 1: Traditional Power versus Modern Power

This table draws out some of the distinctions that can be made in the contrasting of modern and traditional operations of power. According to Michel

Traditional Power A mechanism of power that:
Establishes social control through a system of institutionalised moral judgement that is exercised by appointed representatives of the state and of institutions of the state.
Instils in people the aspiration to achieve a grant of moral worth.
Is located at a defined centre, and is taken up and expressed according to the particular and unitary interests of those who appropriate and monopolise it.
Is developed and implemented from the top down.
Acts to oppress, repress, limit, prohibit, impose, and to coerce.
Acts predominantly on a populous and on defined groups of people.
People are mostly on the outside of and find themselves the subjects of.
Places the spotlight on the centre of power, rendering: i) ever visible the excesses of power that are available to those who monopolise it, and that might be called upon to coerce and to punish. ii) invisible, through a range of exclusionary practices, including banishment, exile, expulsion, and execution, those who are most intensely the focus of its operations.
Employs a technology of power characterised by symbols of influence – including pomp, ceremony, public punishment, and awe inspiring edifices – and mechanisms of surveillance and structures for the policing of peoples.

Foucault (1979,1980,1984), since the latter part of the seventeenth century, these modern operations of power have progressively displaced the operations of traditional power as the primary mechanism of social control in western culture.

Modern Power A mechanism of power that:
Establishes social control through a system of normalising judgement that is exercised by people in the evaluation of their own and each other's lives.
Instils in people the aspiration to achieve a grant of normative worth.
Is located in circuits of shifting coalitions and alliances that have both competing and overlapping interests, featuring relatively arbitrary participation that is forged by specific circumstances that are often of quite a temporary nature.
Is developed and refined at the local level of culture.
People actively participate with in the fashioning of their own and each other's lives according to the constructed norms of contemporary culture.
Acts to disperse a populous by allocating each person a specific location in relation to contemporary norms about life and identity, so contributing to the cellularisation/ individualisation of life.
Recruits people into the surveillance and the policing of their own and each other's lives.
Turns the spotlight onto the lives of individuals, rendering: i) invisible and anonymous the circuits of shifting alliances and coalitions that compose one if its characteristic features. ii) ever visible the lives of those who are its subjects, instilling in them a sense that their lives are always available to general scrutiny and to public evaluation.
Employs a technology of power that is characterised by continuums of normality/abnormality, tables of performance, scales for the rating of human expression, formulae for the ranking of persons in relation to each other, and specific procedures of assessment and evaluation that makes possible the insertion of people's lives into these continuums, tables, scales and ranking systems.

The failures

Because the phenomenon of personal failure has grown so exponentially, I believe it appropriate to now speak of the 'modern failures'. And, in view of the fact that there has been such an extraordinary multiplication of the avenues or routes to failure in recent decades, I believe that it is helpful to group these routes into categories. For example, there are those experiences of personal failure that are the outcome of what might be called 'the lapses' and 'the omissions'. The lapses might include:

a) simple mistakes and errors of everyday life that take place in the context of social relations and that are often considered to reflect a lack of togetherness or social competence;
b) failure to achieve desired ends in regard to personal development objectives;
c) going off track in terms of one's goals for one's life;
d) losing the tour in terms of what is generally conceived of as life's evolving and progressive journey;
e) expressions of life that contradict self-possessed and self-contained presentations of one's identity to the world;
f) unsatisfactory performances of one's assigned social role;
g) general backsliding on the established purposes for one's life;
h) expressions of apprehension while on one's path to true confidence;
i) a glitch in relation to one's efforts to be who one truly is, and so on.

The omissions might include:

a) letting options for self-cultivation to slip past unnoticed;
b) unknowingly foregoing opportunities to realise one's full potential;
c) neglecting to seize upon opportunities that are available to engage in the normalising judgments of self and others;
d) inattention to a range of possibilities for locating oneself and/or others on continuums of development, health and normality;
e) overlooking chances to rank self and/or others on this or that table of performance;

f) inaction in the face of a range of opportunities for extended self-surveillance and for the more precise documentation of one's expressions of life, and so on.

Yet other routes to failure might be grouped under 'the resistances', which are shaped by specific skills of living and knowledges about life that are both historical and cultural, either erudite or local, and that people knowingly and unknowingly engage with. The resistances might be identified in a broad range of actions, including those that reflect:

a) a wilful abandonment of the pursuit of adequacy;
b) an obstinate rejection of aspirations for the achievement of superior status;
c) an obstreperous resistance to the classification of people's lives;
d) a perverse interest in relational forms that are challenging of the narrow legitimated forms of contemporary culture; and, more generally,
e) a headstrong negation of the contemporary emblems of normalcy, including those of 'self-actualisation', 'wholeness', and 'authenticity'.

The sorting of the routes to personal failure into 'the lapses', 'the omissions', and 'the resistances' in the way that I have done here provides an account of just a few of the possibilities in this endeavour. Undoubtedly there are many other routes to failure that might be grouped into yet other categories.[4]

Part Two

Refusal

In the first section of this article, I briefly discussed the development of a modern system of social control that is founded on the practices and the technology of normalising judgement. I contrasted this with a description of a more traditional system of social control that is founded on the practices and technology of institutionalised moral judgement. In this discussion, I linked the development of this mechanism of normalising judgement with the exponential growth of personal failure in recent decades, and gave an account of some of the ever-multiplying routes or avenues to this experience.

There appears to be a direct relationship between the intensity of people's experience of personal failure, and the distance that they have assigned themselves and been assigned by others from the cherished and socially constructed norms for what it means to be a person of worth in our culture. Although the sense of personal failure that is derived in this way can have the effect of inciting people to work ever so much harder to reproduce these norms for what it means to be a 'real' person, this sense of personal failure can also be understood to represent an example of the partial failure of modern power itself. This is the failure of the effectiveness of the sort of power that requires people to reproduce the socially constructed norms of personhood of contemporary culture, that requires them to approximate these norms in their every expression of life.

I will reiterate this point. The experience of personal failure can be considered to reflect the partial failure of a particular system of power, the existence of which is dependent upon its success at enlisting people in the shaping and disciplining of their identities according to these norms – and specifically upon its success at engaging people in the harmonising of their lives with these norms. According to this understanding, the avenues or routes to personal failure that were described in the preceding section of this paper can also come to represent avenues or routes to the sites of people's lives in which not only the partial failure of modern power might be identified, but in which people's opposition to, or refusal of, modern power might become known.

What are the implications of this understanding for practice? When people represent themselves to be a personal failure, in understanding that this might also represent a failure of the effectiveness of modern power, space is opened to identify a range of actions that might be characterised as feats of opposition to modern power, or as acts of refusal of what is being required by it. These feats of opposition and acts of refusal might be those very actions that had set these people on routes to the construction of themselves as personal failures by identity. That is, those actions that have provided people with a route to personal failure have the potential to provide them with avenues for exploratory journeys into other territories of their lives in which their acts of refusal (or acts that might be so constructed) of modern power might be identified and become richly known.

Refusal writ large: refusal as a mode of thought and mode of life

Having engaged with the proposition that a sense of personal failure might also be read as a person's refusal of the requirements of modern power, we might well ask: 'What is the foundation of such a refusal?'; 'What is it that makes this refusal possible?' One answer, albeit a thin one, frequently given in response to these questions is that this refusal is simply the outcome of the direct actions that are undertaken by people in their struggle with, and in their efforts to negate, modern power. Another answer, less frequently given, is that this refusal is simply the outcome of a chance event or a misreading of the expectations and requirements for life that are sponsored by the norms for personhood of contemporary culture. Answers such as these are relatively unsatisfying. The first provides little appreciation of what it is that provides the foundation of acts of refusal – it is as if these refusals, these struggles, come out of thin air! And although the second answer provides a viable account of the starting conditions for acts of refusal, it provides no explanation of why a refusal that is the outcome of a misreading or chance event can be enduring despite the ongoing and broad discouragement of this.

Upon questioning the vacuous nature of these accounts of people's acts of refusal, a range of notions about human nature are often evoked in efforts to more adequately explain them. These refusals are often represented as expressions of people's 'real' identities, of their 'true' consciousness, of the elements of their 'authentic' selves, of the 'essences' of their humanity. Apart from the fact that these naturalistic claims – that is, claims that these acts of refusal are founded, in one way or another, in people's natures – lead to very narrow inquiries about human action, there are many grounds for questioning these claims. For example, attention can be drawn to the rather conspicuous and intimate relationship between such 'naturalistic' accounts of identity and the manufacture of the contemporary norms for personhood that provide a platform for modern practices of normalising judgement. Conceptions of elements and essences that are considered to be of human nature, and of the ideal ways of life that unencumbered human nature is a rational expression of (for example, self-actualised, self-realised, self-possessed, and self-contained ways of life), have provided fertile conditions for the construction of these norms - the rule of the contemporary norm is invariably expressed under the ruse of 'natural law' and 'rational rule'. Because it is claimed that these norms represent the 'truth' about human nature, about what is 'natural' and 'universal', the options for questioning these norms through critical reflection are significantly reduced.

Apart from drawing attention to the conspicuous and intimate relationship between naturalistic accounts of identity and the manufacture of the contemporary norms for personhood, there are other grounds for challenging these claims that represent these acts of refusal as expressions of human nature. For example, many questions can be raised about how it could ever be possible to sustain any account of identity, including of human nature, that would not be a social, cultural and historical product, and that would be outside of language and beyond the systems of understanding and discursive practices that shape people's existence.

When considering acts that might be understood to represent a refusal of the requirements of modern power, another response to the above questions ('What is the foundation of such a refusal?'; 'What is it that makes this refusal possible?') is informed by the observation that if a person is refusing to live the life that s/he is assigned to live, and is not being the person whom s/he is required to be, then s/he is living a different life and is being someone else, whom s/he might not have significantly been before – that s/he is pursuing some alternative identity projects that do not so comprehensively reproduce the norms for the favoured individualities of our culture. In these circumstances it could be expected that explorations of this 'different life' and this 'someone else' could be revealing of other modes of life and thought that are also social, cultural and historical. It is in this sense that we might find, in the shadows of failure, other knowledges of life and practices of living that do not so directly reproduce the cherished norms of the contemporary world.

This is a conclusion that leads to broad inquiries into these other knowledges of life and practices of living, inquiries that are not only identifying of these knowledges and practices, but that also contribute to these being richly known. These inquiries provide a foundation for people to more significantly familiarise themselves with and to pursue alternative identity projects that do not so completely reproduce these norms for personhood.

The following account of my conversations with Judy provides an example of a therapeutic inquiry into the knowledges of life and practices of living that are to be found in the shadows of failure.

Judy

Judy, a woman in her mid-forties, who lived solo, was referred to me by her cousin, Aerin. Aerin had been concerned about Judy's state of despair for a considerable time, and had made numerous attempts to counsel her over this. From time to time she had also encouraged Judy to seek professional help, but rarely was Judy even minimally responsive to this encouragement. On two or three occasions, at Aerin's behest, Judy had attended groups associated with the human potential movement. She had also read numerous popular psychology texts that Aerin had recommended.

Recently, after renewed efforts on Aerin's part in persuading Judy to seek professional help, Judy had consented to see a counsellor. Aerin had then called me on her behalf to make an appointment.

Judy: So, that's it Michael. Aerin talked me in to coming to see you. But I said to her, and I still think its true, that I'll be wasting your time. I'm a chronic case. I'm hopeless. Everybody knows it.

M: So why did you agree to come to see me?

Judy: Because lately I've been feeling totally miserable, and I just thought I had nothing left to lose. And then there's Aerin. As you know, she was pretty enthusiastic about the idea.

M: You said that you were a chronic case. A chronic case of what?

Judy: Look, I'm really a dependent personality. Everyone can see it! You wouldn't believe what a dependent person I am. And nothing ever turns out right with what I do. I'm telling you, I'm always just incompetent.

M: Well, could I ask …

Judy: No Michael, I know what you'll say, but these realisations are true. What I am saying about myself, it's really true. Aerin's tried to convince me that it isn't so, that I am wrong about myself, and you'll probably try to do the same. But I know that you are all just trying to make me feel better. I can tell. But it won't work.

M: You said that you were too dependent and incompetent. Too dependent in relation to what? Incompetent in relation to what?

Judy: Now that's easy to answer. How much time have you got? I just can't make up my mind about things like competent people do. I am so totally changeable. I'm so easily influenced by others. I'm not at all strong in myself, like everyone else seems to be. This is just one of my big failures. I don't get done what any reasonably independent person would. And I know I am a fair burden to my friends and family. Do you want more, because I could fill you in on …

M: Well that gives me a reasonable idea. In decision- making you haven't achieved a reasonable level of competence. You've failed to be strong in directing your own life. You don't make it onto the independence scale. And on account of your dependence, you are a burden to others. How's my understanding?

Judy: Well that's a relief!

M: What's a relief?

Judy: You haven't tried to talk me out of these realisations. Or tried to tell me that I am really okay after all, which I am just sick of hearing.

M: I also understand that you have had these negative realisations about yourself for a long time.

Judy: Yeah. It seems like I've felt this way forever. Yeah, practically forever. It's painful. But there is no escaping from the facts, is there?

M: How do you mean it's painful? Would you say more about what it is like for you at those times that these negative realisations are most strongly present. How do they affect how you feel? How do they affect what you do?

Judy: Surely you could figure that one out.

M: I could have a fair guess about how such negative realisations would effect my life, but we are different people.

Judy: Well I could hardly say that they make my life a picnic! I get totally stressed out ... I get wrung out. I am always tired out.

M: I take it that these realisations are pretty taxing of you.

Judy: I think they totally sap my motivation, in every way that you could think of. I get to feel so defeated about all of my efforts to do something about my life, in whatever I do to try to get myself together. I get to feel so defeated in my efforts to achieve some independence and to be a competent person.

M: These negative realisations are obviously hard taskmasters. When they are strongly present they have you working hard on yourself, they have you engaged in lots of efforts to shape up, and yet they also discourage these efforts that you are making. Is that it?

Judy: Yeah. When I am not feeling totally defeated, that is.

M: I would like to understand more about what these negative realisations demand of you when you are not feeling totally defeated. Could you give me some practical examples of what they have you doing?

Judy: Lots of things. Lots of things. I have tried lots of things to fix myself. I have read all of these self-help books and found out more about what I could be and what my life would be like if I had even an ounce of competence. And I've tried personal development exercises that are recommended, and just wind up feeling worse. More inadequate! More dependent! Now how useless am I? And, the same thing happened in the personal growth classes I went to. I'm sure that these are good for lots of people, but for me, well, they just showed me what I already knew about myself.

M: What's that?

Judy: That I am a hopeless case.

M: Well that's really something!

Judy: What? That I'm a hopeless case!

M: No. That you kept putting yourself through all of these hoops when the outcome was so unsatisfactory to you.

Judy: But I think I've pretty well given up now. Not totally, I suppose, because I am here talking to you. But I'm close to it, I really am.

M: You said that you have pretty well given up. Do you mean that you have stepped back from some of these efforts to get yourself together?

Judy: Yeah, I guess so. In some ways I am ashamed to admit it. It's not a real good sign, but what else can I say. I feel pretty hopeless.

M: How have you managed to step back from all of these efforts?

Judy: Managed!!! It's like I said, I am a hopeless case!

M: But you did leave some stones unturned in your efforts to improve yourself. And you could have found yet more bookstores, and new personal development exercises to apply yourself to. And you could have found other programs to enrol in.

Judy: No, forget it. Just forget it. It is just all too much. I am fed up with it all. I'm just not going to do it anymore.

M: You sound quite firm about this decision. At some point I would like to hear more about these steps that you have taken in turning away from all of these efforts. But right now I would be interested to know where these steps come from.

Judy: Where do they come from? I am just tired of having to get 'THERE', to achieve 'THIS', and to make 'THAT' of my life! Where does this come from? It is just about a little bit of self-preservation. Surely you don't think … (trails off)

M: Self-preservation! What is it that you are preserving?

Judy: I don't know. How would I know? The word just jumped right out of my mouth!

M: It's interesting. You have taken steps to turn away from all of these efforts to get yourself together, and you said that this was about self-preservation.

Judy: Yeah.

M: When you think about the steps that you have taken in turning away like this, and about how these steps are based on self-preservation, what pictures or images come to your mind.

Judy: Like what?

M: Like maybe images of a person who you have known, or of your own life, or of who you are. Or maybe certain realisations about what's been important to you in your life.

Judy: I can't think of anything in particular.

M: Or maybe images of a film that you have seen, or of a book that you have read. Or images of a character in a film or a book. Or images of anything else.

Judy: I can't say that … Well … Wait … Yes … When I really think about your question, my mother's sister, Aunt Clara, comes to mind. She's dead now.

M: How come?

Judy: How come she's dead!

M: No. What's your understanding of why her image comes to your mind?

Judy: I'm not sure, except that I do know that she was different to the rest.

M: Was she into self-preservation?

Judy: Yeah. I guess she was. When people tried to push her into doing things, she just wouldn't co-operate. No matter how hard anyone tried to persuade her to do something, if it wasn't something that she had come to herself, and that seemed right to her, it just wouldn't work. She would become totally immoveable. If anything was pressuring her, she would turn away, and she would just turn off.

M: Sounds like she was a pretty determined person.

Judy: Yeah. My Aunt Clara didn't react well to pressure. It's not that she didn't do things, because she did interesting things that weren't always conventional. In fact, the more I think about her the more I realise just how unconventional she was. She had her own way of getting things done, and … yeah, I don't think that she was at all interested in measuring up to anyone else's opinion.

M: You said that she had her way of getting things done. Was she always doing things independently of others?

Judy: No. Not at all! That's not the picture I meant to give of her. It was the opposite. What I remember is that she always liked doing things with people. She really valued doing things jointly with other people. I also remember that she was never fussed about what lengths she had to go to get something done, as long as she was doing it together with others, and as long as there was no pressure on her to conform to anyone else's expectations. She was really patient, and she didn't even mind how long things took to get done if she believed they were important. She wasn't even discouraged if things didn't work out as planned in the end.

M: Where does the piece about self-preservation come in? It doesn't sound like she was big on the 'self' part of this.

Judy: I mean self-preservation in a different way. I think that what I mean is that … Well, I suppose in that Aunt Clara would always preserve the life that was important to her. For example, she was there for the company and the journey, and nothing would separate her from this.

M: What's your understanding about what this says about what Aunt Clara valued most?

Judy: Let's see. I think that doing things with others in … There's a word for it, but I just can't get it. Um …

M: In collaboration, in partnership, in …?

Judy: In partnership! That's the word.

M: When I asked you about these steps in turning away from all of the efforts you'd been making in your efforts to …

Judy: To shape up?

M: Yeah. When I asked you about what these steps were based on, you said that they had a basis in 'self -preservation', and you then started to tell me about your Aunt Clara. Is it possible that your life and Aunt Clara's life are linked in some way? For example, could your lives be linked in a particular sort of self-preservation, and in the priority that you give to being in partnership with others?

Judy: I don't know. I have never really thought about this.

M: Does the idea that your lives might be linked around self-preservation and what was important to her strike any chords for you?

Judy: Yeah. I guess so. Yeah, I can see that in a way that it does fit. In some ways at least. Yeah, I can see that. I've never really thought about this before, and it is taking a bit to get my head around it. And …

M: What is it like to think that your life and Aunt Clara's life might be joined in some ways?

Judy: (tears welling) It's big.

M: It's big?

Judy: (sighs) Because who would have ever thought that I could be following in her footsteps. I would never have thought this.

M: But you are thinking this now?

Judy: (more sighs and tears) Yeah, and I feel very emotional about it.

M: Do you know why?

Judy: I think because it is such a relief. You know, she was a special woman, and to think about the ways that she went about her life, the ways that I could really stand back and appreciate … I don't think I'm saying this very well, but it's a relief to think that some of the ways that I go about life might fit with the ways that she went about life. Well, who would have thought … (more tears, trails off)

M: Which realisation do you like best. This one or the one about you being a hopeless case?

Judy: (laughing and crying) This one, this one, this one.

M: (also laughing with tears) I think I heard that.

Judy: So did I. And I have to tell you. I am amazed to hear it!

M: Could we talk more about what you were saying about Aunt Clara and the theme of preservation, and about her commitment to partnership, and about her ways of being in life? I ask this because I think this could help us to clarify the manner in which you are linked to these values and principles in the way you live your life. It also might throw a different light on those conclusions you'd reached about being a dependent person, and about not being able to get done what any reasonably independent person might get done. That's if you want to do this, of course.

Judy: It sounds good to me.

M: Such a conversation could also provide us with some ideas about avenues for you to extend on these themes in the way that you go about your life and your relationships. But before we get into this, could you tell me how this is going for you?

Judy: I have to tell you that right now I am feeling a bit light for the first time since, well, since a very long time ago. I feel warmed too. I'm feeling this physically right now. My life has seemed such a dead ended and cold place in many ways.

M: In that case I guess it would be a good idea to continue in this direction. But we only have a little time left before the end of this meeting. In the time that we have left, I'd like to ask you about what you were saying at the beginning of our meeting about dependency and about not getting done what you should be getting done.

Judy: Okay.

M: If there is a significant link between these ways of living, and your Aunt Clara's sense of self-preservation and the values that she had about partnership, what is your guess about how your life and your relationships would go if this link became stronger for you?

Judy: I guess that I would be pretty wary of making changes that weren't in partnership with other people. Yeah. And I would always want to be inclusive. I don't just mean being open to being with others, but I would want to be active in inviting them into my life in lots of ways.

M: And what about what you said about Aunt Clara's sense of time? Something about timelines not being so important to her.

Judy: I guess that if I didn't let timelines frustrate me, if I didn't let them get the better of me, then I wouldn't give up and feel so hopeless about myself so often.

M: We are going to have to stop here. I have taken some notes about what you have said about this, so we could take it from here at our next meeting.

Judy: That would be good.

Discussion

So began a series of conversations that were richly describing of the form of self-preservation that was strongly featured in Aunt Clara's life, of the system of values that shaped her expression of this self-preservation, and of the self- and relationship-forming activities that were a characteristic of Aunt Clara's life. In the context of these conversations, Judy began to draw out the multiplicity of ways in which her life and Aunt Clara's life might be linked around these themes, and she took initiatives to thicken these themes in her own life. In the course of our seven meetings, many of Judy's realisations that she was a dependent and incompetent person were displaced by new realisations about the ethic by which she lived. Like Aunt Clara, this was an ethic of partnership in which what mattered was the value that she gave to doing things in partnership with others, the commitment that she entered into to give whatever time necessary to building foundations for new possibilities in life, and her refusal to be governed by timelines or by short-term goals in these endeavours.

In our last two meetings, at Judy's invitation, we were joined by Aerin and three friends who Judy had believed she'd burdened on account of her 'dependency' and 'incompetence'. Judy and I first caught these visitors up on our conversations and on developments in Judy's life. In doing this Judy shared her newly articulated questions about the idea of independent action, and powerfully described the ethic of partnership that she had been more significantly fostering in her life. Aerin and Judy's friends responded to this with some beautiful reflections on Judy's inclusion of them in her life, and expressed a desire to further explore this ethic of partnership that linked the lives of these women.

At the outset of our meetings Judy had so strongly believed that her 'realisations' about her dependence and incompetence were strictly true. These realisations had prompted her to take a number of steps in an effort to bring her life more into harmony with the norms from which these realisations were derived – norms associated with contemporary cultural notions of independence and competence. In these efforts Judy had intensified her participation in the operations of modern power, and the outcome was a stronger sense of what she had been attempting to reduce – that is, her sense of personal failure. Some understanding of the analysis of the operations of modern power, and the part that these operations might have played in Judy's predicament, made possible new therapeutic initiatives in addressing her sense of failure. These initiatives constituted an alternative identity project. In these initiatives, Judy's opposition to the operations of modern power was identified, as were the modes of life and thought that provided a foundation for this opposition. These modes of life and thought became richly known, and this significantly reduced her susceptibility to participate in the normalising judgement of her own life.

In the next section of this paper, I will introduce a framework that can provide a guide to the development of these alternative identity projects within the context of therapeutic conversations.

Part Three

Alternative identity projects

In previous sections of this paper I have proposed that it is possible to engage with a sense of personal failure in a way that provides for a reading of this as a refusal of modern power. I have also proposed that, in the shadows of this failure, other knowledges of life and practices of living might be identified and richly described. Further, I have suggested that such an inquiry might provide a foundation for people to more significantly pursue identity projects that do not so completely reproduce the favoured individualities of contemporary western culture.

These proposals raise questions about the particularities of how this might be done. What sort of inquiry might contribute to the identification and rich description of not just these acts of refusal, but of the ways of living and thinking that provide a basis for these acts? And how might this inquiry also provide a pathway to the development of a valued sense of self while not so closely reproducing the venerated individualities of our culture?

These are significant questions, because they take us to considerations about the production of life itself, about the manufacture of identity, about the fabrication of the human subject. I believe that some appreciation of the processes of the manufacture of identity to be very helpful in the formation of a therapeutic inquiry that sponsors possibilities for the remanufacture of identity. It is in this context that I will again refer to the work of Michel Foucault. A specific focus of Foucault's work was the history of the fabrication of the human subject, with an emphasis on the constitution of the self as a moral agent. In this endeavour he inquired into the elaboration of one's relationship to oneself and one's life through different eras, and referred to this as the study of ethics.

In his studies, Foucault concluded that, through different eras, there could be identified four aspects in the constitution of self as a moral agent: 'ethical substance', 'mode of subjectification', 'aesthetics', and 'telos'.[5] I will discuss each of these in turn.

Ethical substance

> *Foucault: The first aspect answers the question: Which is the aspect or the part of myself or my behaviour which is concerned with moral conduct? ...*
>
> *Question: But, roughly, for the Christians it was desire, for Kant it was intentions, and for us now it's feelings?*
>
> *Foucault: Well, you can say something like that. It's not always the same part of ourselves, or of our behaviour, which is relevant for ethical judgement. That's the aspect I call ethical substance.*
>
> (Foucault 1994a, p.263)

The ethical substance is that aspect of life that is considered of primary relevance to ethical judgement. This ethical substance is whatever it is about our lives that is our responsibility to manage well. In tracing the history of this aspect of the constitution of the self, Foucault illustrated the way in which what is deemed relevant as the 'ethical substance' changes from one era to the next. For example, for the ancient Greeks it was 'pleasure' that had to be managed well (pleasure was to be moderated, and excesses revealed and reigned in), while for the early Christians it was forms of 'desire', often referred to as concupiscence (desire for the flesh was to be renounced).

In the present era, most understandings of identity are shaped by the modern notion of the 'self'. Although this notion of self is a relatively novel idea in the history of the world's cultures, in most circles in western contexts it is now routinely accepted that this self exists 'in fact', and that it is the source of personal identity. Many cherished beliefs about human nature have been constructed around this taken-for-granted 'truth', and very often people will baulk at any questioning of the veracity of these beliefs.

The aspects of life that are now usually considered of primary relevance to ethical judgement are categories of the self: one's essential 'feelings', one's deepest 'desires', a personal 'property', an individual 'resource', a human 'need', an intrinsic 'attribute', an innate 'drive', an unconscious 'motive', and so on. It is the management of these modern categories of the self that we are now required to occupy ourselves with – one's feelings are to be kept faith with, one's desires are to be liberated, personal properties are to be cultivated, individual resources are to be put into circulation and capitalised on, human needs are to be satisfied, intrinsic attributes are to be expressed, innate drives are to be modulated, unconscious motives are to be revealed. These new understandings about ethical substance herald a shift from moral considerations to normative considerations.

Mode of subjectification

> *The second aspect is what I call the mode of subjectification (mode d'assujettissement), that is, the way in which people are invited or incited to recognise their moral obligations. Is it, for instance, divine law that has been revealed in text? Is it natural law, a cosmological order, in each case the same for every living being? Is it rational rule? Is it the attempt to give your existence the most beautiful form possible?* (Foucault 1994a, p.264)

The second aspect of the constitution of the self as a moral agent is the 'mode of subjectification' (not 'subjugation'). It is the mode of subjectification that provides the mechanism through which people are encouraged or required to recognise their moral obligations in regard to the management of the relevant ethical substances. For example, in the judgement of one's management of the relevant ethical substances, is one to refer to: divine laws; to the laws of nature; to rational rule; or to particular systems of values and principles – for example, like the system of values that is expressed in certain religious or humanist narratives, in ecological conceptions of life, or like the system of values that is associated with the concept of life as a work of art.

According to Foucault's understanding of the principle modes of subjectification in the ancient Greek and early Christian eras, for the ancient Greeks it was through aesthetic values that one might appreciate the obligations that must be observed in the pursuit of pleasure. And for the early Christians it was through divine law that one might know what obligations s/he has in the management of desire. It is through attending to these obligations that one becomes virtuous.

In considering the modern era, we could assume that it is principally through the discourses of 'truth' that are associated with socially constructed norms, and that are expressed in 'rational' rule, 'natural' law, and 'personal rights', that people are invited to recognise not their moral obligations, but their normative obligations. These are normative obligations in: the expression of their essential feelings; the liberation of their desires; the cultivation of their personal properties; the realisation of and in the capitalising on their personal resources; the satisfaction of their individual needs; the expression of their intrinsic attributes; the modulation of their innate drives; and the revealing of their unconscious motives. It is through this preoccupation with, and the conscientious application of oneself to, the 'truth' of who one is that one becomes virtuous, and might achieve an exemplary life.

Asceticism

> *The third one is: What are the means by which we can change ourselves in order to become ethical subjects? ... What are we to do, either to moderate our acts, or to decipher what we are, or to eradicate our desires, or to use our sexual desire in order to obtain certain aims such as having children, and so on – all this elaboration of ourselves in order to behave ethically. ... That's the third aspect, which I call the self-forming activity – asceticism in a very broad sense.* (Foucault 1994a, p.265)

The third aspect of the constitution of self as a moral agent is what Foucault referred to as 'asceticism', and he gave this term a broad definition. Asceticism is about lifestyle. It is about the self- and relationship-forming activities[6] that one engages in when observing the obligations that one has to become an ethical subject in the pursuit of an ethical existence. It is through these self- and relationship-forming activities that one elaborates an identity and a life that can be considered ethical.

The self- and relationship-forming activities emphasised by Foucault were what he called the 'techniques of life' and the 'techniques of the self': the techniques that one uses in order to recognise oneself as an ethical subject. These techniques of life and of the self include all of those self- and relationship-forming activities that one might engage in to:

a) moderate one's pleasures (which, as with the ancient Greeks, included the sort of personal aesthetic and political practices that would provide a foundation for caring for the city);
b) decipher and to modulate one's desires (which, as with the early Christians, included practices of confession); or to
c) be true to one's feelings, liberate one's desires, cultivate one's properties, capitalise on one's resources, satisfy one's need, express one's attributes, realise one's potential, reveal one's motives, and so on (which in the modern era, as discussed in an earlier section of this article, include practices of normalising judgement which are shaped by a wide range of technologies of assessment and evaluation).

In contrasting the constitution of the self through these and other eras, it was Foucault's purpose to show that the self-forming activities that one engages with are hinged to what is considered relevant as an ethical substance and to specific modes of subjectification. The form that one would give to one's life when engaging in the creation of self as a work of art would not be the form that one would give to one's life if one was engaged in the 'renouncing' of the self, or in the 'discovery' of the self. These represent very different self-forming activities, and, for that matter, very different relationship-forming activities. Although Foucault emphasised these self-forming activities as techniques of the self, they also shape the formation of one's relationships with others, and with communities of people. For example, he discussed how, for the ancient Greeks, techniques for the moderation of pleasure included 'caring for the city'.

Telos

> *The fourth aspect is: Which is the kind of being to which we aspire when we behave in a moral way? For instance, shall we become pure, or immortal, or free, or masters of ourselves, and so on? So, that's what I call telos.* (Foucault 1994a, p.265)

The fourth aspect of the constitution of self as a moral agent is 'telos'. Telos is about the mode of being or the kind of being that we aspire to be when we are behaving in a moral way, or, in modern times, in ways that provide us with a grant of normative worth.

Telos expresses the goal or the end-point that one seeks to arrive at in one's identity project. For example, it might be an aspiration to achieve a life that is one of self-mastery, of purity of being, of godliness, or a beautiful life that is artistic in form. It might be a goal to achieve salvation or an eternal life, or perhaps an exalted reputation. Alternatively, under the guidance of modern day rationality, it would more commonly be an aspiration to achieve a life of self-possession, of personal fulfilment, of self-actualisation, or one that reflects a pinnacle of liberation of the self.

Discussion

In tracing the history of the constitution of the self as a moral agent through the various eras of western culture, Foucault sought to bring to light the extent to which modern ascetics of living exclusively sponsor a mode of being that is linked to norms about life and identity. He also sought to bring to light the extent to which these norms are assigned the status of 'truth'. On account of this, the modern mode of being becomes one that is defined entirely in terms of knowledge. Foucault traces this development to Descartes' agenda to establish 'the attainment of a mode of being where doubt was no longer possible, and where one could finally know'. Foucault raised a fundamental question about this:

> *After all, why truth? Why are we concerned with truth, and more so than with the care of the self? And why must the care of the self occur only through the concern for the truth? I think we are touching on a fundamental question here, what I would call the question of the west: How did it come about that all of Western culture began to evolve around this obligation of truth which has taken a lot of different forms?* (Foucault 1994b, p.295)

Foucault's aim in raising this question was to sponsor new explorations in the aesthetics of living. These are explorations that are not linked to this obligation of 'truth' or to a *morality of renunciation, but as an exercise of the self by which one attempts to develop and transform oneself, and to attain to a certain mode of being* (p.294). This exercise of the self requires 'a rejection of a priory theories of the subject' and is associated with the perception that the human subject is not a 'substance' but a 'form'. The therapeutic practices described in this article provide an opportunity for people to separate their lives from this 'obligation of truth' that is associated with normalising judgement. These practices also provide an opportunity for people to engage in self- and relationship-forming activities that are instead linked to a range of other considerations, including non-institutionalised moral and aesthetic considerations. Amongst other things, this can provide the foundation for the development of a moral agency that is not linked to the sort of moral judgement that is obliged by specific social, religious and legal institutions that have authoritarian and disciplinary structures. This is a moral agency that is linked to what Foucault referred to as an 'autonomous ethic of living'.

Part Four

Practice implications

In the opening section of this paper I referred to my longstanding interest in the problems of people's lives, and placed the focus of this present discussion on the subject of personal failure, which I understand to be an ever-growing phenomenon. I proposed this phenomenon to be closely associated with the rise of modern systems of social control that are based on practices of the normalising judgement of persons, rather than moral judgement. As there is now a multiplicity of avenues to personal failure, I constructed a classification of some of these: the lapses, the omissions, and the resistances.

I then suggested that personal failure might also represent a failure of the sort of modern power that requires that people manufacture identities that are in relative harmony with our culture's socially constructed norms for personhood, not identities that are discordant with these norms. But, more than this, I suggested that this failure might be testimony to people's acts of refusal of modern power. On the basis of this, I sought to demonstrate that these acts of refusal do not come 'out of the blue', but are founded on modes of life and thought that do not so completely reproduce the cherished individualities of our contemporary world. This took the focus of this discussion to some explorations of the extent to which these acts of refusal might represent alternative identity projects that contribute to options for people in the remanufacture of their identities. These reflections about the manufacture and remanufacture of identity prompted further considerations about the fabrication of the human subject. It is in this context that I referred to Michel Foucault's work on the constitution of self as a moral agent.

At this juncture, I will provide a map for inquiry into personal failure that I hope readers will find useful in their own explorations of the practice implications of the ideas raised in this paper. This is an inquiry of the sort that:

a) makes possible the identification of people's refusals of the requirements of modern power;

b) contributes to the rich description of modes of life and thought that do not so completely reproduce the sanctioned individualities of contemporary culture; and

c) provides a basis for the remanufacture of identities that provide an alternative to those identities linked to modern rationality and the discourses of truth, and that provide the foundation for the modern phenomenon of personal failure.

This map is presented in eight distinct stages, although in the actual practice of this inquiry there is considerable blurring of these stages, and rarely does this inquiry take the form of a strictly linear progression. As well, seldom is each stage of this inquiry accorded equal significance, and therapeutic conversations will loiter in some of these stages longer than in others. It is my hope that this map will provide some assistance to therapists in uniquely locating people's failures in life, in the identification of the many routes to failure, and of the many routes away from it. Although I hesitate to present such maps out of a concern that they may become prescriptive of practice, I take consolation in the fact that maps do not specify the destination of our therapeutic conversations, or the routes taken by them, and that they can be helpful in opening up, to intentional investigation, neglected territories of people's lives.

Although the illustrations of therapeutic inquiry that I give in this article focus on 'lapses' and 'omissions' as points of entry to the remanufacture of identity, these are not the only sources of failure, and not the only routes available to alternative identity projects.

In presenting this map, I am not suggesting that all experiences of personal failure be responded to in this way, or that all experiences of personal failure are the outcome of the operations of modern power. There are many contexts of life that contribute to an acute sense of personal failure, including those in which people are subject to trauma. However, I believe that even in the case of significant trauma, this 'failure conversations map' can be relevant insofar as impinging traumatic memories render people more vulnerable to the excesses of normalising judgement. In these circumstances the failure conversations map can be brought together with other traditions of inquiry that are effective in addressing the effects of trauma on memory systems.

Failure conversations map

1. Failure in relation to

This first category of inquiry is structured by questions that are revealing of the expectations, norms and standards that people believe they have failed to adequately reproduce in their acts of living. These are the expectations, norms and standards that make it possible for people to conclude that they are inadequate, insufficient, incompetent, useless, and so on.

In the practice illustrations already given in this chapter, these questions included:

to Max: *You said that you had reached a conclusion that you were personally inadequate, and that you feel like a failure. What is it that you feel inadequate in relation to? What is your sense about what you have failed to achieve?*

to Judy: *You said that you were too dependent and incompetent. Too dependent in relation to what? Incompetent in relation to what?*

2. Response to failure

This second category of inquiry is structured by questions about the actions that people have initiated in their efforts to address these failures and inadequacies – actions taken in relation to one's own life and one's relationships in efforts to measure up, to meet these expectations, norms and standards. These questions encourage people to describe these actions, which often take the form of extraordinary psychological gymnastics. In response to these questions, people usually provide an account of a range of operations, processes, programs, methods, procedures, measures, regimens and treatments that are taken up in the disciplining of one's self and of one's relationships.

In the practice illustrations already given in this chapter, these questions included:

to Max: *You also said that you have been trying to make it as a counsellor in the agency. In finding yourself falling short of the mark, what have you been doing? What have you been doing in your pursuit of adequacy?*

to Judy: *How do you mean it's painful? Would you say more about what it is like for you at those times that these negative realisations are most strongly present? How do they affect how you feel? How do they affect what you do?*

I would like to understand more about what these negative realisations demand of you when you are not feeling totally defeated. Could you give me some practical examples of what they have you doing?

3. Unique Outcomes

This third category of inquiry is structured by questions about the potential unique outcomes that might be identified in the context of this inquiry. These unique outcomes might be evident in people's:

a) expressions of a degree of acceptance of aspects of the state of affairs of one's life that do not fit with these expectations, norms and standards;

b) responses that don't fit with these expectations, norms and standards, but over which people are not giving themselves the hard time they could be giving themselves, and in

c) actions that might constitute some form of refusal of, or that might convey a sense of not being wholly available to, or that might be questioning of , these expectations, norms and standards.

In the practice illustrations already give in this chapter, these questions included:

to Max: *This leaves me curious about something. You have a sense of not making it, and you are giving yourself such a hard time, but you have kept going, and you haven't quit. You have nearly quit, but you haven't. Have you discovered something that encourages you, that makes it possible for you to keep going? Or is it just that you let up on yourself at times? How do you keep going?*

to Judy: *You said that you have pretty well given up. Do you mean that you have stepped back from some of these efforts to get yourself together?*

4. Foundations of action

This fourth category of inquiry is structured by questions that are identifying of the actions that are associated with these refusals. These questions make it possible for people to distinguish the personal feats that have provided the basis for these achievements. These are achievements that have provided a platform for refusals not just of the expectations, norms and standards, but also of all of the operations, processes, programs, methods, procedures, measures, regimens, and treatments that are associated with these socially constructed norms. In the practice illustrations of this chapter, these questions included:

to Max: *What do you do that keeps you in touch with this appreciation of the people who consult you? What steps do you take in this?*

to Judy: *How have you managed to step back from all of these efforts?*

You sound quite firm about this decision. At some point I would like to hear more about these steps that you have taken in turning away from all of these efforts.

5. Ethical Substance (bottom-line consideration)

This fifth category is structured by questions that invite people to define what it is that is expressed in the steps that they have taken in establishing a platform for these refusals. This inquiry is identifying of those aspects of life that people judge to be of primary relevance in regard to how they lead their lives, and for which they experience a degree of responsibility to manage well. The questions of this category of inquiry encourage people to identify these aspects of life in 'experience near' terms. For Max this was 'integrity', while for Judy it was 'self-preservation'.

In the practice illustrations already given in this chapter, these questions included:

to Max: *What are you expressing in your interest in the lives of the people who consult you? And in these steps that are shaped by this interest?*

If you were to name what is important to you that is a foundation for this interest and these steps, that is one of those bottom-line things, what words would you come up with? Words that would describe what you would feel comfortable about having to answer for in your work?

to Judy: *You sound quite firm about this decision. At some point I would like to hear more about these steps that you have taken in turning away from all of these efforts. But right now I would be interested to know where these steps come from.*

6. Mode of subjectification (system of rules/body of values and principles)

This sixth category of inquiry is structured by questions about what it is that people refer to as a guide to them in the management and expression of whatever it is that they consider to be of primary ethical relevance in their lives (bottom-line consideration). For example, in response to these questions, people might make known:

a) certain values and principles associated with different systems of belief, religious or otherwise, and which may, in some contexts, be accorded the status of 'rules' or 'laws' of living; or

b) certain values and principles that are shaped by culture and class specific narratives about the 'good life'.

These questions also open inquiry into the different ways in which people are oriented to these values and principles. For example, people may have a sense that observing these values and principles in the management of their ethical substance is a matter of preference, or of responsibility, or of duty, or that this is a matter of obligation.

In the practice illustrations already given in this chapter, this inquiry was initiated by the questions:

to Max: *Integrity! Now I would like to ask you some questions about what it is that guides you in expressions of this integrity. ... Would that be okay?*

to Judy: *When you think about the steps that you have taken in turning away like this, and about how these steps are based on self-preservation, what pictures or images come to your mind?*

What's your understanding about what this says about what Aunt Clara valued most?

7. Asceticism (self- and relationship-forming activities)

This seventh category of inquiry is structured by questions about the identity elaborating and life-shaping activities that people engage in as they go about observing the responsibility that they have to become an ethical person (or 'subject') in the pursuit of an ethical existence. These are questions about people's self- and relationship-forming activities. These activities relate to lifestyle considerations, and are the outcome of people's efforts to manage whatever it is that is deemed to be the relevant ethical substance according to the system of rules/body of values and principles that is identified in the preceding inquiry into 'mode of subjectification'.

In the practice illustrations already given in this chapter, this inquiry was introduced by the questions:

to Max: *When you are experiencing this integrity, and feeling more or less at one with the values that we have been discussing, what is that like for you? Are you giving yourself a hard time? Or is it different?*

We've been tracing out the ways in which this integrity and these precious values and beliefs are implicit in much of your work. We've also been talking about how this shapes your relationship with the people who consult you, and about how this might be touching of the lives of these people. ... Would you be interested in a conversation about how this integrity and these values might be given a more overt presence in your counselling work?

What's your guess about how you would be responding in these meetings if this integrity and these values that we have been discussing were more explicitly present for you, and more openly expressed by you?

to Judy: *If there is a significant link between these ways of living, and your Aunt Clara's sense of self preservation and the values that she had about partnership, what is your guess about how your life and your relationships would go if this link became stronger for you?*

8. Telos (goal or desired end state)

This eighth category of inquiry is structured by questions about people's goals for their lives, about what they are aspiring to in their efforts to act in an ethical way, about the desired end states of their lives. Telos can also be an account of the kind of being that one believes one is a candidate to become.

For Max, telos was 'to achieve a life of goodness'. For Judy it was 'to craft a principled existence'.

In therapeutic conversations subsequent to the ones described in this article, I introduced this inquiry with the questions:

to Max: *Max, thanks for catching me up with some of the recent developments in your life that fit with this integrity and the values that are important to you. What does this say about what your life is about, about what you are out for in life?*

to Judy: *I understand that you have developed an even stronger sense of the ways that your life and your Aunt Clara's life are linked around themes of self-preservation and partnership values. What is your guess about what Aunt Clara would have said about her goal in life, one that you might also share with her?*

In the foregoing discussion I described a 'failure conversations map' that provides a guide to addressing the contemporary phenomenon of personal failure. In presenting the eight categories of inquiry of this map, I drew from practice illustrations already given in this chapter. These practice illustrations were taken from the transcripts of my conversations with Max and Judy. I will now provide a third and last illustration of the application of this map in my meetings with Denise, a twenty-four-year-old woman, and her parents, Katherine and Gordon. I encourage readers to keep the failure conversations map before them as they follow the transcript of my conversations with this family, to use this to chart the course of these conversations and to identify the questions that initiate each stage of inquiry.

Denise, Katherine and Gordon

I introduced myself to Denise and her parents, Katherine and Gordon, in the waiting room. All three were apprehensive, and it was clear to me that Denise and Katherine had been crying. Denise's movements were slow, and our journey to the interviewing room seemed a long one. When we were seated, Gordon and Katherine informed me of Denise's lack of enthusiasm over this appointment with me, and began to speak of their concern for her. In response to this, I consulted Denise about her understanding of this appointment, and the circumstances of her attendance. With an economy of words, she flatly informed me that although she'd had no wish to attend this appointment, she had not felt compelled to do so, and had decided to do this for her parents' sake.

I asked Denise if it would be okay by her for her parents to fill me in on their concerns for her, or whether she would prefer to speak to her understanding of these concerns. To present an alternative, I wondered aloud if she might rather speak to her own agenda for our meeting, and perhaps about any concerns that she might have for her parents. In response, and again with great economy of words, Denise said that it would work best for her if Gordon and Katherine were to speak.

In the next ten minutes I learned that Denise had been diagnosed with schizophrenia some years ago after a series of psychotic episodes, had been trialed on several different major tranquillisers, and had been hospitalised on half a dozen occasions. Although Denise was now on a medication that had relieved her of some of the more troubling aspects of her psychotic experience, her general quality of life was poor – she was quite isolated and withdrawn, often despairing, at times quite desperate, and felt generally hopeless about her future. I asked Denise if she thought that her parents had an accurate account of how things were for her, and she nodded in affirmation.

Katherine and Gordon had made the appointment to meet with me after a recent suicide attempt on Denise's behalf. To their knowledge this was her fifth attempt, and the most life threatening of them all. Following Denise's recovery from this, she confided to them that she felt herself to be failure as a person in every way imaginable, and that she believed that she would never get a life together.

Gordon: So that's why we made this appointment Michael. There just has to be something else that we can do.

Katherine: Yes, Denise doesn't have a very good time of life. Do you honey? (turning to Denise, who is now in tears). I know she feels such a failure, but she's not. And we love her so much.

Denise: (crying softly)

Katherine: I know that you didn't want to come here, and that you did it for us. (turning to Michael) Getting her out of her bedroom is very difficult on any occasion.

M: (turning to Denise) Your parents have now filled me in on what they are concerned about. I have done my best to check these concerns with you, and understand from your response that these concerns are mostly accurate. Would it be okay for me to ask you a few questions?

Denise: (nods)

M: Can you confirm what your parents are saying about feeling that you are a failure?

Denise: (shrugs, then nods in affirmation)

M: Can you talk about this?

Denise: (still crying softly) Don't think I can.

M: Would it be okay by you for me to ask your mum and dad about what they think this is like for you?

Denise: It's okay.

M: (to Katherine and Gordon) Would you say more about your understanding of what this is like for Denise?

Gordon: Time and again we have seen Denise set out to make something of her life, and time and again she has crashed, and everything has come undone. So, I think that this has convinced her that she is a failure as a person.

Katherine: We feel so much for her when we see these expectations crushed. We try to reassure her and tell her that it is okay, that there will be other days, but this doesn't work anymore. Now there isn't anything that we can do at these times to make her feel better (Katherine and Denise's eyes meet, and they are both in tears).

M: You mentioned expectations. What are these expectations that Denise feels that she is failing?

Katherine: Just the usual. That she will get herself together, have a life.

M: Expectations for what sort of life?

Katherine: You know all of those things like being independent, achieving her goals. Being able to handle herself in social situations, like having it together socially. Having a relationship, and maybe a career. All of these things.

Gordon: Yeah. Achieving her best potential.

M: Where do these expectations come from?

Katherine: I'm glad that you asked this question. Because it's not just from us, is it Gordon?

Gordon: We hear these expectations all of the time. People are always giving us opinions about what would be good for Denise. About what she could be doing, about what we could be doing. About what they would be doing if they were us and Denise was their daughter, and about what Denise would be doing if she was their daughter. It goes on and on. Mostly it is all pretty subtle, mostly inferences. It is everywhere, and I know that Denise has had her fair share of it.

Katherine: It is everywhere. We've tried not to join in, but we've done it too. I mean we have also put these expectations onto Denise. (turning to Denise) Haven't we?

Denise: (clearly engaged by what she is hearing, nods in affirmation)

Katherine: We know it's not helpful. But it is so hard not to do this when we want so much for you.

M: What's this like for you and Gordon? How do all of these expectations affect how you feel about yourselves as parents? Do these expectations affect your own opinions of who you are as Denise's parents?

Katherine: I know that I don't feel too good about it. Gordon feels this too. We don't like to admit it, and we keep trying, but I think that we both feel like failures as parents. I hope it is okay to say this (turning to Denise), and that it isn't upsetting to you. But Denise doesn't have this sense of being a failure alone. We all have it, but just try to pretend that it isn't there.

M: Gordon?

Gordon: (sighs) Yeah it's true. We don't know where to turn with this. For sure we can't speak to other parents about it. They all seem to be doing so fine (sighs again).

M: You might not be surprised to hear that I meet with a lot of people who have failed a lot of expectations and prospects for their lives. In fact there is so much that can be failed that, some time ago, this got me interested in collecting an account of the possible failures. It would be helpful to me in my conversations with you if we could compile a list of the expectations and prospects that you sense you have failed. Who knows, there might be some new ones!

Gordon: (smiles) I could be part of that.

Katherine: (also smiling) Me too.

M: Denise?

Denise: Yeah. I could help out with that.

M: Great! Let's get started.

Over the next thirty minutes, Denise, Katherine and Gordon assisted me to compile a list of the expectations and the prospects for their lives and relationships that they had a sense of failing to achieve. We also worked together to identify some of the sources that were sponsoring of these expectations and prospects, and discovered these in a range of routinely offered opinions, judgements, conclusions, attitudes, viewpoints, inferences, evaluations and taken-for-granted assumptions about what life is all about. Gordon, Katherine and Denise concluded that virtually all of these were unsolicited.

I then took the opportunity to interview these family members about the effects of these expectations on their lives and on their relationships, and about how these had shaped their conclusions about their identities. As this conversation evolved, Denise began to participate more fully. Apart from other things, these expectations held Denise in suspense. These expectations had her constantly assessing whether her thoughts and actions were real enough, mistrusting most of what she thought and did, questioning everything about her life, and worrying about whether she was coming across as a together person. The expectations had Katherine permanently on duty trying to make things better for everyone, judging herself negatively as a mother and a woman, always appraising and weighing her words and deeds, and engaging in a reckoning of her performance at the end of each day. The expectations had required of Gordon that he be vigilant in his assessment of the adequacy of his words and deeds (did they fit), and had significantly isolated him from friends and workmates.

At the second meeting we compared the list of failed expectations that was composed in our first meeting with a master list that I had been compiling over some years. We discovered that most of the failed expectations on their list were already present in the master list (although they did present variations of two of the items on this master list that I entered as subvarieties). We also discovered that there were many other expectations that Katherine, Gordon and Denise could have subjected themselves to, but hadn't. I wondered aloud about why it was that they hadn't made their lives available to more of these expectations, and why it was that they were not giving themselves the hard time that they could be giving themselves. Gordon, Denise and Katherine found my questions amusing and informed me that they simply hadn't thought of some of these expectations (and that if they had then they wouldn't have had a life at all), and that the others they considered just plain ridiculous.

This review had a dramatic effect on our conversation. Denise, suddenly quite animated, offered that not only had she not made herself available to many of the expectations of the master list, but that she had also 'dropped' some that she had been available to. These were those expectations about being a more productive person. She had decided that there was no way that she could measure up to these, and she no longer experienced such discomfort over this. 'After all', Denise said, 'I am entitled to a little relaxation and fun'.

M: How did you step back from these expectations?

Denise: Just did.

M: It seems to be a pretty big just did. Could you say a little more about what went into this just did?

Denise: Well … Er … It was using my mind.

M: What makes it possible for you to use your mind in this way?

Denise: Well it's like this. I have realised that sometimes I am able to use my mind to say 'no' to these expectations. It's like I've got, now what is it I've got? Let's see. Um ….

Katherine: Is it like willpower? Like having a strong will.

Denise: Yeah. That's it. That's right. That's the word I am looking for. It's willpower.

M: Is willpower something about your life that is important to you?

Denise: Yeah. I guess it is. But I lose it.

Katherine: I think that she always prided herself in it.

M: (to Denise) What is it that guides how you use this willpower?

Denise: I don't know. I don't know. Umm. It's something for sure. What do you think Mum?

Katherine: I think that in lots of ways you are a very accepting person. And you also value understanding. This has shown up many times before. It is like you have these principles that you won't budge on. Way back as far as I can remember, there have been so many times when you wouldn't be reacting to some of the things that you heard like lots of other people would, like everybody would expect, but you would hang in, and keep listening to what was going on. Even when hanging in was possibly hurtful to you, and our hearts were going out to you, you would keep trying to understand what was happening for people.

M: You talked about Denise's accepting and understanding ways, and said that these were principles.

Katherine: Yeah. I would say they are principles. (turning to Denise) You would stand by these principles of understanding and acceptance. Even when we were worried about you getting hurt, you wouldn't budge in this. Whenever we managed to put our worrying aside, it was always somehow refreshing to see you doing this. It was different. Wouldn't you say so Gordon?

Gordon: I agree with Katherine. I've seen this too, many times. Even when you were just a little kid this acceptance and understanding meant a lot to your grandfather, who was losing his way through brain degeneration, and no-one else had much patience for him.

M: Denise, what do you think of this? Do you relate to what your mum and dad are saying about these principles?

Denise: I haven't thought much about it.

M: Are you thinking about it now? Or are you thinking about something else?

Denise: I'm thinking about it. Let's see … Yeah I think it is right.

M: In that case, so far I understand that you used your willpower to get free of some of these expectations, and that your principles of understanding and acceptance guided you in this. How does that sound to you?

Denise: Kinda good.

M: Why would you say kinda good?

Denise: Well, this makes me feel just a little bit better.

M: Would it be okay with you for us to talk about what your life looks like when this willpower is available to you, and when it is being guided by what is important to you?

Denise: Yeah. But mum and dad could help. Couldn't you? (glancing in parents' direction)

Katherine: Well, for a start, when this is all working for her, she is not harassed by time like the rest of us. And I know that people around her don't have to put on such a brave face about things in their own lives that are not working out. I have noticed that they can just let go a bit. They don't have to be so uptight. Maybe because Denise is accepting of other people's complications, of their quirks, they can be more accepting of them as well.

Gordon: It is like when things are working for Denise, she has this ability to provide a bit of a haven for others. I can think of quite a few people that I reckon have found this quite a relief.

M: A haven! Now that presents me with a powerful image. Denise, what pictures of your life are coming to you as you listen to your parents' words?

Denise: Nice ones. Well … they are a bit hard for me to talk about. But I do like them.

M: Do you think it would be helpful if these pictures stayed with you, and if you had more like these?

Denise: Yeah.

M: Why would you say this would be helpful?

Denise: These pictures might make me feel better about myself, and that would make a big difference.

M: What sort of difference?

Denise: I maybe wouldn't get so worried and upset.

M: You'd like to talk more about these pictures of your life? For us to draw them out more?

Denise: Yeah.

Katherine: I think this has been very affirming of Denise. And I have been having lots of realisations as well. These are going to help, particularly with the sense of failure. I mean to help get free of this. For all of us.

M: Gordon?

Gordon: Yeah. I think that we should talk more about this. You know, when you think about it, when you really sit back and think about it, you realise our daughter really is an original. She really is! And for her to know this more, well, that would be fantastic.

Katherine, Gordon, Denise and *Michael*: (all profoundly and visibly moved by this wonderful description of one of Denise's central attributes – 'an original')

M: An original! That is really something!

Discussion

I met with Denise, Katherine and Gordon on eight further occasions over a twelve-month period, and then twelve months later for three more occasions. The conversations had in these meetings contributed to a rich description of the:

a) principles that guided Denise's expressions of willpower;

b) ways of being in the world that didn't conform to everyone else's expectations, and for which Denise became a champion;

c) skills of living that were associated with these ways of being in the world;

d) unique aspirations that Denise had for her life: no longer for a 'normal' life, no longer for a 'productive' life, but for what Gordon described in our third meeting as a 'life of honour'.

Over this time, these conversations provided Denise with a basis for new explorations in self- and relationship-formation. She became generally less stressed, more prideful, and felt less vulnerable to the sort of insecurity that would make her prey to the hostile voices (auditory hallucinations) that had been so unsettling to her in the past. With this improvement in her quality of life she became more socially adventurous. Hopelessness was displaced by a sense of her life unfolding.

As an outcome of these meetings Gordon and Katherine also reported significant progress in regard to the lowering of their general stress levels. They both experienced a 'steadiness' in themselves that had been elusive, felt less vulnerable to the opinions and expectations of others, and said that they were no longer on 'tenterhooks for seventy percent of the time'. They were more able to take upsets in their stride, and became less inclined to 'double guess' the responses of others to their words and actions.

In providing this account of my conversations with this family, I want to emphasise that I am not suggesting that we were directly addressing whatever it is that schizophrenia is. Nor am I suggesting that the work that we did together displaced other approaches to this phenomenon, including those that featured biochemical understandings and the use of medication. However, it is my understanding that it is the sense of being an abject failure to be a person in terms of our culture's cherished ideals about what this means – for example, like attaining high levels of self-possession and self-containment – that recruits people with this diagnosis into extraordinary mental gymnastics in their efforts to be real (by normative standards) and that builds a foundation for a highly stressed life. This renders these people highly vulnerable to acute episodes and to a deteriorating course in life. Over the course of our meetings, Denise was significantly freed from these gymnastics and from the normalising judgement associated with them. In the stead of 'realising her potential' and all of the normative prescriptions associated this, she embraced a 'life of honour'.

Part Five

Further considerations and ethical implications

In the last section in this paper I first address a couple of misconceptions about what is being proposed in the critique of modern power that is featured in this paper: that is, the idea that:

a) this critique and the actions informed by it will have the effect of freeing people from false conceptions of who they are and make it possible for them to look to their 'genuine' interests, and to become who they 'truly' are; and that

b) such a critique of power is synonymous with the denunciation of all operations of power, and with the notion that all power relations can and should be eradicated.

Second, I revisit and further develop the discussion of the small 'p' political implications of this modern analysis of power for therapeutic practice. This subject was touched on in the introduction to this paper, but I believe the importance of these implications render them worthy of reiteration. Third, I review the sort of personal and community ethics that are sponsored by the critical approach to the fabrication of lives featured in this paper. I then close with a discussion of the approach to professional ethics that is informed by the ideas and practices explored in this paper.

Life as constituted

The notion of 'acts of refusal' discussed in this paper is not associated with a proposal that such actions free people from a 'false' consciousness of who they are. And it is not associated with the idea that such actions will make it possible for people to look to their genuine interests and derive a knowledge of who they 'really' are, a knowledge that will render them less vulnerable to power.[7] Rather, this notion of 'acts of refusal' is associated with the idea that life and identity is inevitably constituted, not given, and that such refusals will be linked to possibilities to constitute life in other ways; that the identification of such refusals will introduce possibilities for people to engage with alternative identity projects, in which they might:

a) prioritise expressions of life that are linked to other identity categories;

b) investigate other values and principles by which to shape these expressions of life;

c) survey other self- and relationship-forming activities; and to

d) explore other goals for their lives.

It is through these alternative identity projects that people become familiar with other modes of life and thought that will also be social, cultural and historical products. The further exploration of these modes of life and thought provides people with opportunities for creative reengagements with their own histories.

Not to denounce power

A further comment about this subject of modern power; to represent Foucault's critique of the operations of modern power in the way that I have here is not to denounce normalising judgement as a system of social control. Nor is it to propose that a system of social control based on institutionalised moral judgement be erected in its stead. In the recent history of western culture there can be found many examples of the part that normalising judgement has played in the challenging of the excesses of institutionalised moral judgement and, to the contrary, of the part that moral judgement has played in challenging the excesses of normalising judgement. To critique modern power is not to characterise modern power as bad, and traditional power as good, or to propose a return to the more traditional structures of power that have been significantly supplanted by the operations of modern power. Further, to critique modern power in this way is not to:

a) denounce all operations of power;

b) propose that all power relationships can and should be eradicated; or to

c) deny the utility and effectiveness of the operations of modern power in the fashioning of modern lives, in the building of personal capabilities, in the installation of a range of capacities, and in the perfecting of the skills of living that are the hallmark of life in contemporary western culture.

Rather, in representing Foucault's critique, I have described some of his efforts to unmask the operations of power of 'modern' culture for which concealment is one of its conditions of possibility, and to bring to light some of the specific hazards and limitations of this system of social control. It was Foucault's hope that this would encourage us to: *acquire the rules of law, the management techniques, and also the morality, the ethos, the practice of the self, that will allow us to play these games of power with as little domination as possible* (Foucault 1994b, p.298). In the context of this critique of modern power, Foucault was not employing the word 'games' in a pejorative sense, nor suggesting our participation in power relations to be a frivolous consideration.

In this article I have sought to describe and illustrate some of the ways that this analysis and critique of modern power has been highly relevant to me in the development of therapeutic practices that I have found to be effective in checking the excesses of normalising judgement. Although there are many implications of the analysis of modern power for therapeutic practice, in this article I have chosen to especially focus on the relevance of this to my work with people who construct themselves to be a failure by identity.

Antidote to despair

In this paper I have addressed just some of the implications, for therapeutic practices, of an analysis of modern power which is drawn principally from the work of Michel Foucault. This is a system of power that is effective in recruiting people into the disciplining of their own and each other's lives according to socially constructed norms, not a system of power that is dependent upon the constant presence of agents of social control, and that operates through force, coercion, and authority. The operations of this modern power are being played out in virtually every facet of modern life and identity – these operations are now virtually unrestricted in scope and domain (whether it be the domain of family, work, health, education, leisure, etc.).

To reiterate an observation discussed in the introduction to this article, at times this analysis that emphasises the all-encompassing and pervasive nature of modern power has been considered a cause for despair. However, I have always found this analysis of modern power to be both a source of possibility in my work with the people who consult me and, more generally, a cause for hope – an antidote to despair. If the operations of modern power are everywhere to be perceived, and are dependent on our active participation, then opposition to its operations is everywhere to be encountered, and new opportunities to refuse its requirements of us are ever present.

It is this understanding of the operations of modern power that highlights the small 'p' political aspects of all therapeutic practice. It also brings with it a range of options for small 'p' political action through the development of specific therapeutic practices that are identifying of opposition to, and/or refusals of, the requirements of modern power. This can lend a new significance to what it is that we do in the name of therapy. If we are restricted to a classical analysis that conceives of all operations of power as traditional in form, with clearly defined centres, top-down in the application of its technology, and acting through agents of social control to prohibit, limit, restrict and to coerce, then the range of actions available to us to counter power is significantly narrowed.

In regard to traditional operations of power, opposition is usually characterised by processes of appeal that are ratified in constitutions and guided by rule and law, or with forms of social dissent, which can include significant individual acts of resistance and the co-ordinated struggle of groups of people. If we conceive of all operations of power according to these classical or traditional conceptions, and if considerations of big 'P' political action provides the only recourse to challenge the excesses of these operations, we are vulnerable to discouragement, weariness, despair, resignation, and a paralysis of will. This paralysis of will is the outcome of the fact that, in the context of this classical analysis of power:

a) a relatively narrow range of political actions are deemed relevant as effective counter-measures to the operations of power;

b) those political actions that are deemed relevant as effective counter-measures to the operations of power will have little impression on modern power, which has become the dominant partner in the establishment of social control in contemporary western culture;

c) so many expressions of life that might represent acts of opposition to the operations of modern power, or a refusal of its requirements, are rendered inconsequential.

In these circumstances, responsibilities that we have to oppose the operations of power weigh heavily, and it becomes all too easy to fall to 'neo-liberal fatalism', and to assume that there is nothing that we can do about the institutions and the operations of power.

As previously stated, to emphasise the possibilities, within the therapeutic context, of small 'p' political action that is associated with the analysis of modern power is not to disclaim the presence of more classical or traditional structures of power and the relevance of social dissent. Undoubtedly there are macro and local operations of a power that is institutionalised in form, and that do act to prohibit, to regulate, and to oppress. For example, there are those operations of power that are present in race relations and in the subjugation of indigenous peoples, in gender relations and in the oppression of women, and in the power relations of heterosexual dominance and the disqualification and marginalisation of gay, lesbian and bisexual identities. However, in these contemporary times, even in many of these institutionalised structures of power, there is an ever-increasing dependence on social control through the normalising judgement of persons, and the classical operations of force and coercion are usually reserved for those occasions when the limits of modern power to establish social control are reached.

Ethics of living

The complicity of normalising judgement in the conclusions that people reach about being a failure by identity is a theme that can be traced through the whole of the discussion of this article. In drawing attention to this complicity, in questioning the excesses of normalising judgement, and in engaging in explorations of identity that are challenging of the disciplines of the self and relationship that are associated with normalising judgement, it is at times assumed that what is being proposed is an 'unexamined life' in which 'anything goes'. For, it is sometimes asked: 'If one is not engaged in the judgement of their own actions against universally accepted notions about life, how could it be possible for one to have an examined life?'

However, an unexamined life is not what is being proposed. In fact, to the contrary, what is being proposed is a critical approach to the fabrication of lives founded on self- and relationship-forming activities that are informed by non-institutionalised moral[8] and aesthetic considerations (in contrast to self- and relationship-forming activities informed by normalising judgement). In the context of the therapeutic practices described in this paper, people are provided with an opportunity to refuse normative criteria in the judgement and the justification of their activities, and to instead explore the consequences of these activities in regard to self- and relationship-formation founded on a range of other considerations, including non-institutionalised moral and aesthetic considerations. This focus on the consequences of one's activities in the shaping of one's life and relationships provides fertile ground for the development of strong personal and community ethics.

Professional ethics

I do not believe that it is possible for us, as therapists, to join the people who consult us in these explorations of the ethics of living without being confronted with new questions about the ethics of our own practices. And it is through these questions that we become aware of the extent to which ethical practice is an achievement. In fact, as we become more aware of this, it is invariably the case that these questions make it more difficult for us to attain ethical practice. This I believe to be a significant development, for to engage with these questions has the effect of reversing a trend in which ethical practice in the professional disciplines has become increasingly undemanding. This is a trend in which being ethical is simply achieved by fitting our work out with a few rules and regulations in combination with some helpings of 'boundary speak', and by finding justification for our practices by referencing these to a modern rationality. This is a rationality that is built on taken-for-granted and routinely accepted universal psychological 'truths' about life, about 'human nature', about relationships, and about the family – by the idea that possession of these truths make it possible for us to see the 'evident', to apprehend the world 'as it really is'.

In regard to the rules and regulations that are considered to represent the ethical code of our professional disciplines, although I am not proposing that we can do without some of these, this code does provide a very thin account of ethics. To be ethical in our practice we simply have to do what we are obliged to do, and there are many circumstances in which simply doing what we are obliged to do by such codes cuts across and compromises personal and community ethics. And the outcome of referencing our practice to modern day rationality is that our work can be 'ethical' without any attention whatsoever to the development of our actual therapeutic practices and of the consequences of these practices in the lives of the people who seek consultation.

Our practical engagement with the challenges raised by these questions about our ethics undermines the prospect of constructing an ethical practice that simply privileges the rules and regulations of professional codes, and that is hinged to universal truths. These challenges take us to another version of ethics, a version of ethics that is not passively received but one that is the outcome of our activity. This is an activity in which we find ourselves exercised and stretched, in which we are constantly:

a) reviewing the bottom-line considerations of our practice;

b) appraising the values that we are giving to our work;

c) exploring the specific self- and relationship-forming actions that are shaping of our practice and of our lives;

d) reflecting on this activity with a mind to the aspirations that we have for our work and our lives.

It is my hope that we will have the opportunity for an ever-more significant engagement with the challenges raised by these questions about ethics, and for the further development of these ethics. I believe that this is what is required of us in order to practice well. Amongst other things, I believe that this ethical activity positions us to:

a) acknowledge and manage the political and aesthetic choices that we are faced with in our therapeutic conversations;

b) render these efforts in the management of these political and aesthetic choices visible to the people who consult us;
   establish which therapeutic practices are more likely to be honouring of the values that are set by the context of our work when people seek our help to alleviate their suffering;

c) reflect on the actions that we undertake in the name of therapy, and to take new initiatives in developing structures to monitor the effects of these actions on the lives of the people who consult us, and on our own lives;

d) explore ways of taking up the special responsibility that we have in regard to the consequences of what we say and do in the name of therapy;

e) take what is identified in these reflections and explorations into the re-shaping and reinvigoration of our own practice.

Conclusion

In this paper I have focussed on failure as a contemporary phenomenon, the development of which is deeply rooted in modern systems of social control. I have observed that failure is becoming increasingly available to people, and have underscored the extent to which this is a subject of fascination for me, one that I believe worthy of significant exploration. I have suggested that some investigation of the lapses and omissions that provide people with avenues to personal failure can lead to the identification of people's refusal of the requirements of modern power.

Further, I have proposed that this inquiry can contribute to a recognition of, and to the rich description of, other knowledges of life and skills of living that can be more significantly embraced by people who seek consultation over a sense of personal failure. These are knowledges of life and skills of living that do not directly reproduce those associated with the requirements of modern power. I visited Foucault's account of the manufacture or constitution of identity in the history of western culture, and proposed that this be employed in the structuring of therapeutic practices that contribute to the remanufacture of identity. Some illustrations of these practices were provided

In the course of our work we will continue to meet with people who, like Paul, Judy, Denise, Katherine and Gordon, are encountering the chill of personal inadequacy, the anguish of personal insufficiently, and the hopelessness and desolation associated with the spectre of personal failure. There is an irony associated with this, for these people will be seeking help from the same 'human science' professions that have played a central role in the development of this phenomenon of personal failure. The modern disciplines, including psychology, social work and medicine/psychiatry, have been instrumental in the production of the ideals and the technology of normalising judgement that is substantially of 'human science'. Because of this, I believe that we have a particular responsibility to further our understandings of the operations of modern power, and to develop therapeutic practices that will expand possibilities for the identification, the acknowledgement, and for the rich description of self- and relationship-forming activities that are non-normative. These are those self- and relationship-forming activities that are constituting of identities that deny aspects of modern rationality and elements of what Foucault referred to as the 'regime of truth'. In the context of our work, success in sponsoring these self- and relationship-forming activities will contribute to the further development and appreciation of diversity in lifestyle and will simultaneously have the effect of moderating the dispersal and cellularisation of lives that is the hallmark of modern power.

I will close by inviting you, the reader, in your conversations with the people who consult you, and with family members, friends and colleagues, to play with the ideas expressed in this paper and to speak about the unspeakable – about failure, inadequacy, insufficiency – in ways that open possibilities for alternative experiences of identity.

Failure conversations exercise

I have for a time been introducing the 'failure conversations' map to workshop participants. I have also encouraged workshop participants to explore, in small group contexts, therapeutic practices relevant to the application of this map.[9] The focus of these explorations is on skills development. I have always believed the ongoing development of therapeutic skills to be a significant responsibility for therapists, and, in the context of my teaching, have sought to emphasise the fact that such development is not an overnight achievement. The skills required in building therapeutic conversations are relatively sophisticated, and, as in the cultivation of any faculty, this sophistication is achieved through practice, practice, and more practice.

In the first place, this practice won't always go easily. In the development of any skills that will take therapists into new territories of practice, degrees of frustration, awkwardness and discomfort are to be expected. In teaching contexts I often inform workshop participants that if they do not experience some degree of trepidation and apprehension in the skills development exercises that I introduce then it is unlikely that they are venturing into new territories of practice.

Ahead of engaging in exercises that structure explorations of maps of therapeutic conversations, and that have a focus on skills development, practitioners at times have concerns that this will take them into activities that will displace the spontaneity that they experience in their work. However, as practitioners develop the skills associated with these maps for therapy, the apparent conflict between rigour and spontaneity dissolves. There is no conflict between meticulous attention to the development of specific skills on the one hand, and improvisation on the other. Those expressions of life that people describe as spontaneous are founded on social skills that they have had the most practice in developing. As with any activity that requires degrees of sophistication, spontaneity and improvisation in such activity is achieved through rigour in practice, and through meticulous attention to skills development. As this foundation for spontaneity and improvisation becomes established, it is invariably the case that practitioners experience the development of a new comfort of practice. And they usually find that they begin to experience new resonances between these developing therapeutic skills and aspects of their lived experience.

The exercise that I introduce here provides a context for practitioners to explore the dimensions of the 'failure conversations map'. It also provides opportunities for skills development and for the practice of these skills. The structure of this exercise can also be taken into explorations of other maps for therapeutic practice.

Structure

This exercise is usually undertaken by groups of at least four to five people. One person volunteers to be the interviewer, and another volunteers to be interviewed about personal failure. The remaining group members participate as outsider witnesses (White 1995b, 1997, 1999).

There are four stages to the exercise. First, the interviewer interviews the interviewee. Second, the outsider witnesses engage in a retelling of aspects of the stories heard in the first stage of the exercise in a way that renders these aspects more richly experienced and known by the interviewee and interviewer. Third, the interviewer interviews the interviewee about their responses to the retelling of the outsider witnesses. Fourth, the group members join each other in a review of the exercise. It is emphasised that the outcome of this exercise is not the sole responsibility of the interviewer. Rather, it is an expectation that group members will embrace a shared responsibility for the outcome.

Stage one

The interviewee makes him/herself available to be interviewed about a sense of personal failure. This may be an account of the direct experience of the interviewee, or this interviewee may, through role-play, represent the experience of a person who is consulting him/her about personal failure. The interviewer and interviewee take their direction from the failure conversations map – the interview is undertaken in circumstances of transparency in which the interviewer and interviewee explicitly refer to this map as their conversation develops. During the course of this interview, the outsider witnesses are strictly in the audience position.

At any point during the first stage of this interview, the interviewer and the interviewee may call time-out. At these times it is the task of the whole group to attend to the agenda of the interviewee or interviewer who called time-out. There is no limit to the number of occasions upon which time-out can be called for.

Time-out may be initiated for a variety of purposes. For example:

a) The interviewer may request time-out to recruit the specific or general assistance of the group:

'I have a sense of where we might go in terms of the third phase of the failure conversations map, but I feel at a bit of a loss in terms of what might be some appropriate questions. Would you join me in speculating about possibilities for such questions?'

'I am feeling a bit stuck at this point. Can anyone think of some questions that would fit with this seventh category of inquiry?'

In these circumstances, it is the task of all of the group members to respond to the agenda of the interviewer. This includes the interviewee, who can propose questions that s/he believes could be effective in engaging him/her in this therapeutic inquiry. When the interviewer calls time-out, this is not an occasion for the other members of the group to address their own agenda, or to impose ideas on the interviewer about what they believe to be more adequate ways of going about the interview.

b) The interviewee may request time-out to share some ideas with the group about questions that s/he might be asked that would contribute to the further development of the therapeutic inquiry. Or s/he may invite proposals from other group members for such questions:

'I am finding these questions interesting, but I have some thoughts about specific questions that I might be asked that I believe would contribute significantly to our therapeutic inquiry at this point. These are thoughts about questions that might work better for me. I would like to share these thoughts, and talk with you about how they might be taken up in this exercise, and about how these might shape the conversation.'

'I have a sense of what it is that the interviewer is endeavouring to open up. I would like to talk about this, and for us to have a conversation about the sort

of questions that might make it more possible for me to step into this territory of inquiry'

At this time, it is the task of all of the group members to respond to the agenda of the interviewee.

Stage two

The outsider witnesses respond to the interview with a retelling that is usually structured according to the tradition of acknowledgement that is characteristic of 'definitional ceremony' (Myerhoff 1982,1986). During the course of this retelling, the interviewer and interviewee are strictly in the audience position. The retelling of the outsider witnesses does not constitute an account of the whole of the content of the telling of the first stage of this exercise, but is structured according to the following categories of response:[10]

a) Identifying the expression
As you listen to the stories of the lives of the people who are at the centre of the definitional ceremony, which expressions caught your attention? Which ones captured your imagination? Which ones struck a chord for you?

b) Describing the image
What images of people's lives, of their identities, and of the world more generally, did these expressions evoke? What did these expressions suggest to you about these people's purposes, values, beliefs, hopes, dreams and commitments?

c) Embodying responses
What is it about your own life/work that accounts for why these expressions caught your attention or struck a chord for you? Do you have a sense of which aspects of your own experiences of life resonated with these expressions, and with the images evoked by these expressions?

d) Acknowledging transport

How have you been moved on account of being present to witness these expressions of life? Where has this experience taken you to, that you would not otherwise have arrived at, if you hadn't been present as an audience to this conversation? In what way have you become other than who you were on account of witnessing these expressions, and on account of responding to these stories in the way that you have?

The sample questions that I have provided here are for illustration purposes. They give an account of how outsider-witness responses might be organised in order to reproduce the class of acknowledgement that is characteristic of definitional ceremony. Many other questions can be constructed around each of these categories of outsider-witness response.

The retelling of the outsider witnesses is the product of active inquiry, not passive response. The outsider witnesses routinely interview each other about their responses that are shaped by each of these guidelines, and in so doing link and build upon each other's contributions. At any point in this retelling, outsider witnesses may call time-out to request a consultation on their responses. At this time it is the responsibility of the whole group to respond to the agenda of the outsider witness who called for time-out. This outsider witness might invite the other group members to attend to a specific question, or might request general assistance. In this part of the exercise the interviewer and interviewee do not have the option of calling time-out, but instead do their best to respond to the requests and invitations of the outsider witnesses.

There are many purposes for which outsider witnesses might call time-out, and the following examples address just a few of these:

'I called time-out because I wanted some feedback from the interviewee about whether s/he is finding our responses resonant, and if so, to get some reflections from him/her about which responses are the more resonant. I would also like to ask the interviewee about their thoughts on what sort of responses from us might be yet more significantly resonant with their experiences.'

'I would like to get everyone's reflections on some thoughts I have about where I might go in embodying my retelling, and in acknowledging transport. I am not sure whether what I have in mind is going to fit with the tradition of acknowledgement we are exploring here, and whether it is going to be appropriate for me to take this direction.'

'I think that we have moved to a different place in our outsider-witness retelling. I have a sense that we are getting into congratulatory responses,

and that the interviewee and interviewer will think that we are just trying to point out positives, or to impose our agenda. So it would be good to have a conversation about this, and about where we might go to from here that might fit better with our task.'

Stage three

The interviewer interviews the interviewee about their responses to the retelling of the outsider witnesses. At this time these outsider witnesses are strictly in the audience position. It is not the intention of the interviewer to encourage a recounting of the whole of the content of the retelling. Rather, s/he structures this inquiry according to the same categories of response that shape the outsider-witness responses. I will not include illustrations of these categories of response here as I believe it will suffice for me to simply summarise these categories. The interviewer interviews the interviewee about:

a) which expressions of the outsider witnesses caught her/his attention;

b) what these expressions evoked for the interviewee;

c) the resonances that were triggered for the interviewee by this; and

d) the destinations to which this has taken the interviewee.

As in stage one of this exercise, the interviewer and interviewee have the option of calling time-out during this retelling of the outsider-witness responses. When time-out is called by either the interviewer or interviewee, it is the responsibility of the whole group to respond to this person's agenda for doing so.

Stage four

Group members join with each other in a review of the exercise. At this time they all have the opportunity to speak of their experiences of the different stages of the exercise, and to ask each other questions about their respective contributions. This is also a time for the identification, naming, and recording of the general learnings that were gleaned from the exercise, and of the specific questions that were found to be particularly effective in sponsoring inquiry into the various categories of the failure conversations map. This contributes significantly to the further development of the therapeutic skills relevant to the failure conversations map. Avenues for future explorations of this map can also be proposed at this time.

Notes

1. Foucault considered the power relations associated with normalising judgement to be disciplinary in two senses. In the first sense, rather than being a mechanism of repression and oppression, these power relations engage people in the fashioning of their own lives and in the fabrication of their own identities according to norms that have been constructed through the history of the modern 'disciplines'. In the second sense, rather than being prohibitive and restrictive, these modern power relations engage people in the fashioning of their own lives through the 'disciplines' of the self. Because of this constitutive nature of modern power, it is often characterised as being positive in it effects (in contrast to traditional power which acts to negate through prohibition, oppression, and coercion). This characterisation of modern power as 'positive' is not a value judgement.

2. I borrow this term from Paulo Freire (1999), a Brazilian community educator and activist. It was the rise of this phenomenon of neo-liberal fatalism in the health/welfare/counselling/educational/ community development professions that was of great concern to Freire in the last year or two of his life.

3. These technologies are not the 'constructs' of our culture's socially derived knowledges. Rather, they represent practices of power. To quote Foucault (1994a) on the knowledge/power distinction:

   So it is not enough to say that the subject is constituted in a symbolic system. It is not just in the play of symbols that the subject is constituted. It is constituted in real practices – historically analysable practices. There is a technology of the constitution of the self that cut across symbolic systems while using them. (p.277)

4. For example, we might consider categories of 'the chance events' or the 'the mis-readings'. The chance events might include those that provide an 'accidental' foundation for developments in people's lives that would not otherwise have been predicted. These are those chance events that have the effect of arresting routine and taken-for-granted ways of thinking and being in the world, that unsettle unquestioned 'truths' about life, and that are subsequently rejected or disqualified in the context of wider social relations.

   As for the mis-readings, modern power requires that people engage in highly specific ways of perceiving themselves and their relationships. Because of this, people's meaning-making activity is a condition of modern power's possibility. The attribution of meaning to an experience of life is an achievement, not something that is given in the 'nature' of the experience itself, and because this is a social, not individual, achievement – it is the outcome of negotiations that take place in communities of people – there exists the ever-present potential for the generation of 'mis-readings'. What I refer to here as 'the mis-readings' are all of those interpretations of the events of life that provide unexpected outcomes in human action. These are outcomes that do not fit with the grand narratives of human development, and that have the potential to generate alternative knowledges of life and skills of living.

   To put it another way, the attribution of meaning is achieved in the 'play of code and decoding', and many of the interpretations that are arrived at in this play are the outcome of chance mis-readings that are often considered error. However, the fact that life is capable of this error, and the fact that this has the potential to contribute to the generation of other knowledges of life and skills of living, is something that can be celebrated:

   > *At life's most basic level, the play of code and decoding leaves room for chance, which, before being disease, deficit or monstrosity, is something like a perturbation in the information system, something like a mistake. In the extreme, life is what is capable of error.* (Foucault 1994c, p.248)

5. In providing an account of the fabrication of the human subject through the history of western culture, Foucault contrasted shifting themes in these four aspects of the constitution of self as a moral agent. In providing examples of this, I will quote directly from Foucault (1994a):

> *There are both relationships between them and a certain kind of independence. For instance, you can very well understand why, if the goal is an absolute purity of being, then the type of techniques of self-forming activity, the techniques of asceticism you are to use, are not exactly the same as when you try to be a master of your own behaviour. In the first place, you are inclined to a kind of deciphering technique, or purification technique.* (p.265)

> *We can say roughly that along with these sociological changes something is changing also in classical ethics – that is, in the elaboration of the relationship to oneself. But I think that the change doesn't affect the ethical substance: it is still aphrodisia. There are some changes in the 'mode d'assujettissement' (mode of subjectification), for instance when the Stoics recognise themselves as universal human beings. And there are also very important changes in the asceticism, the kind of techniques you use in order to recognise, to constitute yourself as a subject of ethics. And also a change in the goal.* (p.267)

> *In the Christian book – I mean the book about Christianity! – I try to show that all this ethics has changed. Because the telos has changed: the telos is immorality, purity, and so on. The asceticism has changed, because now self-examination takes the form of self-deciphering. The mode d'assujettissement is now divine law. And I think that even the ethical substance has changed, because it is not aphrodisia, but desire, concupiscence, flesh, and so on.* (p268)

6. In referring the culture of ancient Greece, although Foucault argued that *the care of the self is ethically prior in that the relationship with oneself is ontologically prior*, he acknowledged that *the care of the self also implies a relationship with others* and that the *postulate of this whole morality was that a person who took proper care of himself would, by the same token, be able to conduct himself properly in relations to other and for others* (1994b, p.287). Discussion of the implications of Foucault's assertion of the ontologically prior basis of the care of the self, and of the implications of this in terms of one's relationship to others, is beyond the scope of this paper. On account of this, in this discussion of asceticism I have chosen to refer to 'self- and relationship-forming activities'.

7. In fact the proposal for action that is linked to the notion of 'acts of refusal' is one that inverts many of the time-honoured practices associated with modern 'self-development'. Rather than sponsoring a search for 'truth of the self', this proposal encourages action that is in some ways akin to the ancient practices of the *hupomnemata,* a copybook or notebook that came into vogue in Plato's time, and that was *as disrupting as the introduction of the computer into private life today* (Foucault 1994c, p.272). To quote Foucault on this subject of the *hupomnemata*:

   They do not constitute an 'account of oneself'; their objective is not to bring the arcana conscientiae to light ... The movement that they seek to effect is the inverse of this last one: the point is not to pursue the indescribable, not to reveal the hidden, not to say the non-said, but, on the contrary, to collect the already-said, to reassemble that which one could hear or read, and this to an end which is nothing less that the constitution of the self. (1994c, p.273)

8. These are non-institutionalised moral considerations in that these are not considerations obliged by specific social, religious and legal institutions that have authoritarian and disciplinary structures. Rather, the experience of moral agency that is derived in these conversations is linked more to what Foucault referred to as an 'autonomous ethic' of living.

9. Ahead of introducing this exercise in workshop contexts, participants are provided with a handout that summarises the main points covered in this article, and the 'failure conversations map'. Participants are encouraged to look to this handout for guidance for the duration of this exercise. This workshop handout is available on the Dulwich Centre website: www.dulwichcentre.com.au

10. These guidelines represent my practice translations of the definitional ceremony metaphor, and the tradition of acknowledgement that is associated with this. It is not my intention to provide here a comprehensive account of these practice translations, and would suggest that readers who are interested in trying the failure conversations exercise do some preparatory reading on this subject (White 1995b, 1999). I acknowledge that there are many other

practice translations of this metaphor which are represented in other guidelines.

References

Foucault, M. 1973: *The Birth of the Clinic: An archaeology of medical perception.* London: Tavistock.

Foucault, M. 1979: *Discipline and Punish: The birth of the prison.* Middlesex: Peregrine Books.

Foucault, M. 1980: *Power/knowledge: Selected interviews and other writings.* New York: Pantheon Books.

Foucault, M. 1984: *The History of Sexuality.* Great Britain: Peregrine Books.

Foucault, M. 1994a: 'On the genealogy of ethics.' In Foucault, M. 1994: *Ethics: The essential works 1.* (edited by P. Rabinow) London: Penguin Press.

Foucault, M. 1994b: 'The ethics of the concern for self as a practice of freedom.' In Foucault, M. 1994: *Ethics: The essential works 1.* (edited by P. Rabinow) London: Penguin Press.

Foucault, M. 1994c: 'On the genealogy of ethics.' In Foucault, M. 1994: *Ethics: The essential works 1.* (edited by P. Rabinow) London: Penguin Press.

Freire, P. 1999: 'Making history and unveiling oppression' (an interview). *Dulwich Centre Journal*, 3:37-39.

Myerhoff, B. 1982: 'Life history among the elderly: Performance, visibility and re-membering.' In Ruby, J. (ed): *A Crack in the Mirror: Reflexive perspectives in anthropology.* Philadelphia: University of Pennsylvania Press.

Myerhoff, B. 1986: 'Life not death in Venice: Its second life.' In Turner, V. & Bruner, E. (eds) 1986: *The Anthropology of Experience.* Chicago: University of Illinois Press.

White, M. 1987: 'Family therapy and schizophrenia: Addressing the "in-the-corner" lifestyle.' *Dulwich Centre Newsletter.* Reproduced in White, M. 1989: *Selected Papers.* Adelaide: Dulwich Centre Publications.

White, M. 1988/89: 'The externalizing of the problem and the re-authoring of lives and relationships.' *Dulwich Centre Newsletter,* Summer. Reproduced in White, M. & Epston, D. 1990: *Narrative Means to Therapeutic Ends.* New York: W.W. Norton.

White, M. 1991: 'Deconstruction and therapy.' *Dulwich Centre Newsletter*. Reproduced in Epston, D. & White, M. 1992: *Experience, Contradiction, Narrative and Imagination.* Adelaide: Dulwich Centre Publications. Reprinted in Gilligan, S. (ed) 1994: *Therapeutic Conversations*. New York: W.W. Norton

White, M. 1995a: 'Psychotic experience and discourse.' In White, M. 1995: *Re-Authoring Lives: Interviews and essays*. Adelaide: Dulwich Centre Publications.

White, M. 1995b: 'Reflecting teamwork as definitional ceremony.' In White, M. 1995: *Re-Authoring Lives: Interviews and essays*. Adelaide: Dulwich Centre Publications.

White, M. 1997: *Narratives of Therapists' Lives.* Adelaide: Dulwich Centre Publications.

White, M. 1999: 'Reflecting teamwork as definitional ceremony revisited.' *Gecko: a journal of deconstruction and narrative ideas in therapeutic practice,* No.1. Reprinted in White, M. 2000: *Reflections on Narrative Practice: Essays and interviews.* Adelaide: Dulwich Centre Publications.

White, M. & Epston, D. 1989: *Literate Means to Therapeutic Ends*. Adelaide: Dulwich Centre Publications. Republished as White, M. & Epston, D. 1990: *Narrative Means to Therapeutic Ends*. New York: W.W. Norton.